ESSENTIAL TRAINING FOR

SHIFTING ATMOSPHERES

DESTINY IMAGE BOOKS BY DAWNA DE SILVA

Shifting Atmospheres

Sozo (with Teresa Liebscher)

ESSENTIAL TRAINING FOR

SHIFTING ATMOSPHERES

DISCERNING & DISPLACING
THE SPIRITUAL FORCES
AROUND YOU

DAWNA DE SILVA

DESTINY IMAGE® PUBLISHERS, INC.
P.O. Box 310, Shippensburg, PA 17257-0310
"Promoting Inspired Lives."

This book and all other Destiny Image and Destiny Image Fiction books are available at Christian bookstores and distributors worldwide.

Interior design by Terry Clifton

For more information on foreign distributors, call 717-532-3040.
Reach us on the Internet: www.destinyimage.com.

ISBN 13 TP: 978-0-7684-1569-8

For Worldwide Distribution, Printed in the U.S.A.
3 4 5 6 7 8 / 21 20 19 18

CONTENTS

USING THE STUDY GUIDE

Welcome to this life-changing study on *Shifting Atmospheres*. This study guide will walk you through eight interactive sessions that you can engage with individually or in a small group or class setting. For this subject matter, you may find it most beneficial to experience this training in a group setting.

Additionally, you will have five daily reinforcement exercises. These function as a themed, focused Bible study and will help you meditate on and start practicing what you have learned.

In the daily exercises, partner with the Holy Spirit as you engage the questions that follow each of the entries. It will help you to learn how to take authority over atmospheres from a place of peace, love, and joy.

Each daily assignment begins with an *Empowerment Point* that will summarize what you will be reviewing in that day's devotional reading.

Following the *Empowerment Point* is a *Transformation Thought* that reiterates the day's emphasis, *Reflection Questions* for your interaction, and an *Empowerment Prayer* that will help you personalize and seal the truth you have learned.

SESSION ONE

UNDERSTANDING THE SPIRIT REALM

For by him all things were created, in heaven and on earth, visible and invisible, whether thrones or dominions or rulers or authorities—all things were created through him and for him (Colossians 1:16).

There is an invisible realm that influences the visible. We don't need to fear this realm, but we do need to be aware of it. The more free from sin we are, the easier it will be for us to discern this invisible realm and reject the atmosphere's influence. We'll be allowing the Lord to bring up anything in our lives that needs to be dealt with so we can better discern what is going on around us. Reading the Word of God will flex our spiritual muscles and prepare us for battle. Cultivating a relationship with not only Jesus, but Father God and the Holy Spirit will be key for our success in shifting atmospheres.

SUMMARY

There is more to this world than what meets the eye. There are invisible forces influencing us on a daily basis. As believers, we have the ability as sons and daughters of the Most High God seated in heavenly places, to shift the atmospheres around us. Our connection to Father God, Jesus, and Holy Spirit is vital to shifting atmospheres.

In this session, Dawna De Silva addresses the spiritual realm and offers some techniques on how to stay free from the corresponding atmosphere's influence. She helps us differentiate between atmospheres we are experiencing (those we normally face) and broadcasts we are "picking up" from either other people or the spiritual realm around us. Once we identify the atmospheres that are not our own, we can shift them and exchange their influence for the Lord's blessings (love, joy, peace, etc.).

Col 1:16
Eph 6:12
Heb 4:12

Video Listening Guide

We need to shift what the enemy is saying.

a third of the angels fell.

When we forget there is an invisable realm, we start fighting against the visable realm.

Satan is not at war with God. He is at war with God's children.

In the Sozo world, the open doors are: fear, sexual sin, the occult, and hatred.

Unless a Christian believes a lie, he/she will not sin.

We need to stop pausing at the door of Jesus and boldly walk through both to Father God and to Holy Spirit.

Our normal should look like Jesus.

SESSION ONE

Discussion Questions

1. This session was about how there is a visible realm and an invisible realm that influences us. Each of these realms influences us. If you have been aware that this is true, raise your hand. If this is a new concept for you, raise your hand.

2. Have you ever gotten in a disagreement with someone and realized partway through or afterwards that there was a spiritual force enticing you to argue? If you have a story to share, please do.

3. Have you noticed a trend in media and books toward storylines with vampires, werewolves, zombies, and other creatures? Are there any movies, shows, or books that you have seen or read that mimic spiritual realities? Feel free to share. Why do you think these types of stories are so popular?

4. Dawna shared the story about God speaking to her, "We live out our days until the Lord takes His Beloved home" through the book of Job right before she found out her stepmother passed away. Have you ever heard a timely word from God as you were reading Scripture? Could you share a story with the group?

5. In addition to reading the Word of God and allowing God to speak to us through it, Dawna talks about the importance of communicating with Jesus, Father God, and Holy Spirit. If you have realized that people have stronger relationships with either Father God, Jesus, or Holy Spirit and feel closer to certain parts of the Godhead than others, raise your hand. If you have never really thought about this before, raise your hand.

6. Did you have an epiphany when she shared the story about the biker at the end?

7. Are you are familiar with the Sozo ministry? Raise your hand if you are. Part of the Sozo ministry is to identify lies we believe and to close any open doors we have to fear, sexual sin, the occult, and hatred or bitterness. Dawna says, "Find out what it is inside that hooks you so that when Satan comes and talks to you, he can find no fault in you." How important do you think identifying lies, closing open doors, and getting rid of the hooks in you is for succeeding in spiritual warfare? Why?

GOAL

The goal of this exercise is to start the process of identifying hooks we may have and get rid of them with the Holy Spirit's help. This exercise can be repeated as many times as needed.

ACTIVATION

Identifying and Healing Hooks

Toward the end of the video, Dawna led us in a prayer to identify hooks or open doors we may have to sin and to give them to God. We want to go through that prayer one more time and give the Holy Spirit room to bring what needs to change to the surface so we can take care of them.

When we pray and ask God questions, we expect to hear Him right away. It may be in the form of an internal voice or a mental picture. Remember that God wants to speak to us more than we want to hear. Let's say these prayers aloud together.

Ask, *"Holy Spirit, are there any hooks in me?"*

Ask, *"Holy Spirit, what is this hook?"*

Ask, *"Where did this hook come from?"*

Ask, *"Holy Spirit, who do I need to forgive?"*

This next part you can either pray silently or quietly. Say this prayer: *"I choose to forgive [person's name] for what they [did or didn't do] and for making me feel [insert emotions]. I release them from all judgment."* Feel free to add your own words and to pray it back to the Lord.

Now say, *"Holy Spirit, I choose to give this [insert the name of the hook/lie/open door] back to You, knowing that You are all-powerful and You won't give it back. What will You give me in exchange?"* Write down what He gives to you in exchange. This might be a picture, a promise, or a Scripture.

When I was young living in an apt
people upstairs - forgive them for what they did
and release them from all judgement
a baby sitter - Thank You H.S.

Say, "*Thank You Holy Spirit for leading me into freedom and revealing truth to me. I receive what You have given to me in exchange for what I have given You.. Please fill me up with more of You.*"

DAY ONE

THE SPIRIT WORLD

For we do not wrestle against flesh and blood, but against the rulers, against the authorities, against the cosmic powers over this present darkness, against the spiritual forces of evil in the heavenly places (Ephesians 6:12).

WHEN WE DENY THAT THE SPIRIT REALM EXISTS, WE ACTUALLY LEAVE OURSELVES VULNERABLE TO THE FIERY ARROWS THAT ARE BEING SHOT AT US.

Whether we believe it or not, the invisible realm affects the visible. When we talk about spiritual atmospheres, it may seem esoteric; we're not talking about spiritual energy, fairies, aliens, vampires, souls of the departed, or ghosts. We're talking about demonic spiritual beings that have been allowed to hold influence over people and places because of agreements made by man with them. These spirits have hierarchies and their leader is Satan.

According to the Bible, God originally created Satan and the demons as angels, but Satan (originally called Lucifer) chose to rebel against God along with one third of the angels. Because of this, they were banished from heaven. Although God has authority over them, as do Christians through God's power, Satan and his demons can have influence over us. More often than we think, negative words or behaviors from other people (or negative thoughts in our own mind) are actually messages being broadcast by the demonic realm.

When we are unaware of the demonic forces at work, we can mistakenly start fighting one another or believe that every crazy thought that enters our mind is our own. For instance, feelings of depression, hopelessness, lethargy, anger, jealousy, and lust are the antithesis of the fruit of the Spirit and can be demonically inspired. Of course, there are times that we are just grumpy and experience negative emotions and thoughts of our own origin; but the more self-aware we are and the stronger our connection is with God, the easier it will be to tell when the enemy is feeding us an unhealthy thought or feeling.

While our focus should not be on the demonic realm, we should have an understanding of how it works and an awareness of its influence both on us and on the world around us. It is actually quite simple to take authority over the demonic influences around us. The first step is to recognize their influence and to not attribute it to a certain person or thought pattern developing in our mind.

REFLECTION QUESTIONS

On a scale of 1 to 10, how aware are you of the spirit realm?

(8)

What has contributed to your awareness of the spirit realm?

Bible — Christian books, disciple classes, bible studies
BSF Bible Study Fellowship, Int'l - 4 yrs

EMPOWERMENT PRAYER

Father God, thank You that You have all authority over the visible and invisible realm. You know exactly what is going on at any given moment. Thank You for all the times that You have protected me. I know that You are training me to take authority over both my own mindsets and the demonic realm. Would You increase my awareness of what is happening in the spirit realm around me so that I can shift atmospheres and bring heaven to earth?

DAY TWO

CLEAN INSIDE AND OUT

First clean the inside of the cup and dish, and then the outside also will be clean (Matthew 23:26 NIV).

ONE OF THE BEST WAYS TO SHIFT ATMOSPHERES IS TO CLEAN UP YOUR INNER SELF.

Some ways we give legal access to the enemy are through believing lies, partnership with sin, or harboring bitterness/unforgiveness. Agreement with these aligns our hearts with Satan's agenda. When this happens, the kingdom of darkness is empowered and broadcast through us to others. We can stop the enemy's broadcasts by partnering with the Lord's truth and broadcasting His virtues over an area instead.

Breaking free from lies we believe and sin in our lives can be uncomfortable but don't lose heart. God brings our issues to the forefront because He wants us to be healed. He desires to set us free so the enemy can have no legal access over our lives.

Once we are free from sinful patterns, lies, and bitterness towardX0 others, we can see more accurately what is going on around us. Living with sin, lies, and unforgiveness is like wearing tinted goggles that color the way we view life. Breaking free from these will clean the bugs off the windshields of our lives so that we can see the road ahead clearly.

REFLECTION QUESTIONS

Ask God if there are any legal rights the enemy has to harass or influence you. If you hear "yes," ask Him why. Depending on what He says, you may need to repent for believing a lie or for partnering with sin or you may need to forgive someone. Once you do, ask God what truth He wants to reveal to you. (He may show you a picture.) Write down what you hear and see.

Ask God if there is a sinful pattern in your life that He wants to break. Ask Him what your part is. Then ask Him what His part is. Write down what you hear and take action on what He wants you to do.

EMPOWERMENT PRAYER

Jesus, thank You for dying so I could be free, forgiven, and healed. I don't want to live any less than 100 percent free and pure. Would You give me the grace to see any areas where I am not free so that I can work toward wholeness? I give You permission to illuminate my life, clean me out on the inside, and get rid of any hooks from the enemy. Thank You, Lord, for freedom!

DAY THREE

DIGGING INTO THE WORD OF GOD

In all circumstances take up the shield of faith, with which you can extinguish all the flaming darts of the evil one; and take the helmet of salvation, and the sword of the Spirit, which is the word of God (Ephesians 6:16-17).

THE WORD OF GOD IS LIVING AND ACTIVE AND IT IS A WEAPON OF SPIRITUAL WARFARE.

Jesus, our ultimate example, knew the Word of God. When Christ was in the wilderness, Satan tempted Him but was refuted by the Word of God. Satan quoted Scripture but Jesus came back with other relevant verses. Even demons know the Bible and can tempt or torment people through quoting it. The key is to not only know Scripture, but to know God's heart. When we do this, we avoid becoming victims to any lies that might seem "truthful." For example, when we feel hopeless because of a mistake we've made, the truth is that even though we feel guilty, there is grace through Christ and there is *"no condemnation for those who are in Christ Jesus"* (Rom. 8:1).

Beyond being a weapon of spiritual warfare, the Word brings life to our spirits and is a way for God to communicate with us. Unlike other books, it has the very breath of God behind it. *"All Scripture is breathed out by God and profitable for teaching, for reproof, for correction, and for training in righteousness, that the man of God may be complete, equipped for every good work"* (2 Tim. 3:16-17). We may read the same Scripture passage over and over expecting it to impact us the same way and yet the Holy Spirit may prompt us with these same words to reveal a new aspect within the verse.

It is important for us to read the Bible on a regular basis. It gives strength and nourishment to our spiritual beings. Without it, we would be powerless.

REFLECTION QUESTIONS

What is your plan for getting into the Word on a regular basis? If you don't have one, what would you like to be doing? Ask the Holy Spirit what He would like you to do in this next season with the Word.

1st — I read my devotional for that day. it has 3-4 Scriptures - then I go to my bible and reflect on these scriptures and read the power points of the Word!

Is there a friend you could reach out to and suggest texting each other daily about what you read in the Word? Or is there some other accountability measure you could put in place?

Nancy & I speak a lot by phone re: the Lord

EMPOWERMENT PRAYER

Jesus, You have all power and authority and You know how to wield the sword of the Spirit, which is the Word of God. Would You teach me how to use it so deftly like You did in the wilderness? Holy Spirit, thank You for speaking to me through the Word and bringing life as I read the letters on the pages. I give you permission to convict me as I read and to bring attention to what needs to change in my life. Father God, thank You that Your heart is so full of kindness and not condemnation or punishment. You are so good to me.

DAY FOUR

Cultivating a Relationship with Father God

Jesus gave them this answer: "Very truly I tell you, the Son can do nothing by himself; he can do only what he sees his Father doing, because whatever the Father does the Son also does" (John 5:19 NIV).

We really need to know what Father God is up to and what He wants us to do.

Jesus said He only did what He saw His Father doing (see John 5:19). How close of a connection do we have with the Father? When it comes to shifting atmospheres, there is a lot we could be doing. Rather than exhuasting ourselves trying to shift every atmosphere we encounter, it is important to find out what the Father wants us to do.

To build a close relationship with Father God, we need to forsake any lies we believe about who He is. So many of us have had fathers and/or leaders who have wounded us. This may cause us to believe Father God has some of the same traits they carried. It may be a process to uncover lies we believe about Him and replace them with His truth, but eventually, if we keep pursuing truth, we will see Him for who He really is.

If you have any question about what Father God is like, look to Jesus. Hebrews 1:3 says that Jesus, *"is the radiance of His glory and the exact representation of His nature"* (NASB). Jesus also said,

"He who has seen Me has seen the Father" (John 14:9 NASB). Let's pursue getting healed from any father wounds so that we can have a healthy connection with Father God!

REFLECTION QUESTIONS

Pray this prayer: "Jesus, is there any lie I am believing about Father God? Where did I learn this lie? Who do I need to forgive? What is the truth?"

Write down the truth here.

Pray this prayer: "Jesus, is there an attribute You have that I have not seen that Father God also has? What is it?"

Write down what Jesus says here.

EMPOWERMENT PRAYER

Jesus, thank You for revealing Father God's heart to me and for making a way for me to have relationship with Him by Your death on the cross. I am so grateful to You, Jesus. Father God, I want to know You better. I want to have a relationship with You where I can sit next to You and hear what it is You are saying to me. Would You continue to reveal Your heart to me so that I can partner with You to bring heaven to earth? Please show me what You're up to every day so I can know how to best partner with You.

DAY FIVE

CULTIVATING A RELATIONSHIP WITH THE HOLY SPIRIT

If I do not go away, the Helper will not come to you; but if I go, I will send Him to you (John 16:7 NASB).

THE HOLY SPIRIT IS THE POWER THAT LIVES IN US TO HEAL.

It was Jesus's sacrifice that gave us the ability to walk through the veil, to be forgiven, to boldly go before the throne of grace, and to walk up to Father God and say, "Abba Father." This is an amazing gift. But there is a third part of the Trinity that we must not forget. Jesus told His disciples, *"If I do not go away, the Helper will not come to you; but if I go, I will send Him to you"* (John 16:7 NASB). It is important that we cultivate not only a relationship with Father God, but also the Holy Spirit.

The Holy Spirit is the power that lives in us to heal and to do the good works of God. Entire denominations refuse to talk about the Holy Spirit and miss out on His promises. The fruit of the Spirit (see Gal. 5:22-23), which we will talk more about in a later session, and the gifts of the Spirit (see 1 Cor. 12 and 14) are empowered by the Holy Spirit. It is the Holy Spirit that keeps our passion burning for Jesus and empowers us to bring the Gospel to earth.

We can hear directly from Father God and Jesus when we read the Word, but we also need to cultivate a relationship with the third member of the Trinity. The Holy Spirit loves to communicate with us. We need to stop pausing at the door of Jesus and walk through to the unexplored territories of relationship with Father God and Holy Spirit.

REFLECTION QUESTIONS

How do you feel about the Holy Spirit? How do you see His power in your life?

What are some ways you can cultivate your relationship with the Holy Spirit this week?

EMPOWERMENT PRAYER

Holy Spirit, I don't want to exclude You from my daily life. You're the One who empowers me to live the great commission and to do the works Jesus said I could do. You comfort me, You love me, You counsel me, and You make me look more like Jesus. Please speak to me today and help me to be aware of Your presence. Remind me to keep talking to You and thanking You for the good things that You are doing in my life. You are amazing!

SESSION TWO

Tactics of the Enemy

Anyone you forgive, I also forgive. And what I have forgiven—if there was anything to forgive—I have forgiven in the sight of Christ for your sake, in order that Satan might not outwit us. For we are not unaware of his schemes (2 Corinthians 2:10-11 NIV).

There are certain tactics the enemy uses to entice us into losing our focus. Some of these tactics are being afraid of the demonic, believing lies, and harboring unforgiveness toward others. If Satan can bait or move us with these, we may miss out on our God-given assignments. In this session, we are going to heal any places where we aren't living victoriously so that we can say goodbye to the enemy's lies and hello to lasting wholeness.

> *According to the working of his great might that he worked in Christ when he raised him from the dead and seated him at his right hand in the heavenly places, far above*

all rule and authority and power and dominion, and above every name that is named, not only in this age but also in the one to come (Ephesians 1:19-21).

God, being rich in mercy, because of the great love with which he loved us, even when we were dead in our trespasses, made us alive together with Christ—by grace you have been saved— and raised us up with him and seated us with him in the heavenly places in Christ Jesus (Ephesians 2:4-6).

For we do not wrestle against flesh and blood, but against the rulers, against the authorities, against the cosmic powers over this present darkness, against the spiritual forces of evil in the heavenly places (Ephesians 6:12).

SUMMARY

The enemy has certain tactics that he uses to distract us and get us into battles we were not meant to fight. The good news is that once we are aware of these tactics, we will be less apt to fall prey to their strategies and more equipped to stand strong. One of the enemy's tactics is deception—getting us to believe lies about the demonic realm, ourselves, others, and God. Satan is, after all, the father of lies (see John 8:44).

In this session, we will learn about common tactics and lies of the enemy, and how we can overcome them with truth. Jesus said He is *"the way, and the truth, and the life"* (John 14:6) and the Holy Spirit loves to reveal truth to us. There are some powerful tools in this session for recognizing lies and replacing them with God's view of the situation. Don't be alarmed if some lies come to the surface. Be glad that God is bringing them into the light so that we can receive wholeness!

WEEK 2

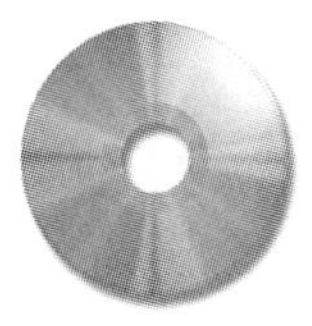

Video Listening Guide

If the enemy can distract us, then we're fighting a battle that's not the right battle.

We must remember that we are Seated with Christ and the very things that are attacking us are coming from an invisable realm that we have authority over.

Fear is one of the biggest tools that the enemy uses against us.

The enemy wants us to believe we are powerless against him.

The enemy wants us to believe lies about: ourselves, others, and God.

Self-sufficiency takes you out of the heavens with Christ and puts you down in the level of fighting man.

The enemy wants your worship rather than you worshipping God.

SESSION 2

Discussion Questions

1. Dawna says that both extremes of focusing too much on the demonic realm and not acknowledging it at all are dangerous. Why is that?
2. What should we be doing instead of focusing on the demonic?
3. Sometimes we might start to feel sorry for ourselves when the enemy is attacking us, and then start to blame God for the attack or for not protecting us, which is exactly what the enemy would like us to do. Have you ever done that?
4. What are some solutions to win the battle over fear?
5. According to Ephesians 6 we are in a war, but what do we learn in Ephesians 1 and 2 that should comfort us?
6. What are some common lies we believe about the enemy?
7. What are some common lies we believe about ourselves that disempower us?
8. What are some common lies we believe about others?
9. What are some common lies we believe about God?

GOAL

We want to expose any lies we are believing about ourselves, others, or God and replace those with the truth so that the enemy does not have a place to hook us.

ACTIVATION

Identifying Lies and Replacing Them With Truth

We want to take some more time to let the Lord bring any lies we are believing to the surface. Let's say these prayers out loud together.

Ask, "*Holy Spirit, is there a lie that I am believing about myself?*"

Ask, *"What is the lie?"*

Ask, *"Holy Spirit, where did I learn this lie?"*

If it was from a person or institution, forgive them. You can pray this prayer out loud quietly or silently. *"I choose to forgive [insert person or institution's name] for teaching me the lie that [insert lie]. I forgive them for [what they did or didn't do] and making me feel [insert how you felt]. As I forsake this lie I release [person or institution's name] and myself from judgment."*

Ask, *"Holy Spirit, what's the truth?"*

Write down what you see or hear when you asked the Holy Spirit for the truth. Only write down the good. You don't have to keep a record of the bad memories, lies you believed, or any forgiveness prayer you prayed.

Judgement w/ Peg

Now ask, *"Holy Spirit, are there any lies I am believing about someone else? What are they?"*

Ask, *"Holy Spirit, what is the truth?"*

Write down the truth.

I have no right to judge
I repent - asked for forgiveness and pleded the Blood of Jesus

Ask, "*Holy Spirit, how would you like me to choose to partner with the truth for this person?*"

Write down what the Holy Spirit tells you.

As Dawna said in this session, sometimes we think we are fighting people, but actually we're fighting against the wounds inside of them. Once we recognize what wounds they have, we can decide not to partner with the actions these wounds produce and partner with God's truth for the people instead.

Now ask, "*Father God, are there any lies I am believing about you? What are they?*"

Ask, "*Father God, where did I learn this lie?*"

If he shows you a person or institution, pray through this forgiveness prayer out loud quietly or silently. "*I choose to forgive [insert person or institution's name] for teaching me the lie that [insert lie]. I forgive them for [what they did or didn't do] and for misrepresenting Your nature. As I forsake this lie I release [person or institution's name] and myself from judgment. I break agreement with this lie. You, Father God, are not like a lot of people, and I let this go.*"

Ask, "*Father God, what is the truth?*"

Write down the truth that you hear or see.

Thought the Father was unreachable
and could only reach Jesus did not pray to
H. S. – only Jesus!

DAY SIX

SEATED WITH CHRIST

But God, being rich in mercy, because of the great love with which he loved us, even when we were dead in our trespasses, made us alive together with Christ—by grace you have been saved—and raised us up with him and seated us with him in the heavenly places in Christ Jesus, so that in the coming ages he might show the immeasurable riches of his grace in kindness toward us in Christ Jesus (Ephesians 2:4-7).

WE ARE SEATED WITH CHRIST AND THE VERY THINGS THAT ARE ATTACKING US ARE COMING FROM AN INVISIBLE REALM THAT WE HAVE AUTHORITY OVER.

There are two extreme approaches to the spirit realm. One is to not acknowledge that it exists and the other is to focus too much on it. If we ignore the spirit realm, we will be susceptible to its attacks and unable to fight back effectively. If we focus on the spirit realm too much, especially on the demonic, we will become afraid and our energy will be spent fighting unnecessary battles.

We must not forget that God is on the throne and that Jesus is over Satan and the spirit realm. Ephesians 1:19-21 says, *"According to the working of his great might that he worked in Christ when he raised him from the dead and seated him at his right hand in the heavenly places, far above all rule and authority and power and dominion."* So there is never a question of who is bigger. Satan and the demons are all created beings.

While demons aren't harmless or stupid, we do not need to fear them. They would like nothing better than for people to be afraid of them. God is on His throne and we are seated with Him in heavenly places (see Eph. 2:4-7). It is from this place that we hear God's instructions, hear His strategies, and do battle. There's no need to fear because God is present!

REFLECTION QUESTIONS

Where do you consider yourself on the spectrum of paying attention to the demonic? What level of fear do you have toward the demonic?

I belive we are in a battle w/ the demonic realm. - I don't over think or dwell on the demonic, but I would not like to be confronted by it!

Ask God if your focus needs to change. If so, how? Write down what you hear from God.

I have the authority to tell the demonic to leave and I don't partner w/ it!

Invite Jesus to give you a vision of Him seated in the heavenlies and you seated with Him. Write down what you see.

EMPOWERMENT PRAYER

Jesus, thank You for reminding me of my position where I am seated in heaven with You. You are high above everything that is seen and unseen. Thank You that I don't have to be afraid because You are living inside of me and You are more powerful than any demon I might encounter. Train me how to reign with You. I want to learn how to partner with You to shift atmospheres over this world.

DAY SEVEN

BELIEVING THE TRUTH ABOUT OURSELVES

But to all who did receive him, who believed in his name, he gave the right to become children of God (John 1:12).

PARTNERING WITH THE LIES WE BELIEVE INSIDE COMPLETELY DISEMPOWER US TO FIGHT.

The enemy has limited power and can only gain it by convincing people to believe lies. Of course, he is sneaky so people don't always know where the lies come from. This is why so many people dismiss demonic voices or impressions as their own thoughts. If the lies feel true, it makes them easier to believe. Three categories of lies we are going to look at in this study are lies about us, lies about other people, and lies about God.

When we received Jesus, we became children of God (see John 1:12). As God's children, we have a myriad of privileges. Our special authority is comparable to earthly princes and princesses that have special privileges because of their royalty. The more we understand the truth of who we are, the less likely we will succumb to the lies of the enemy about our identity.

The enemy likes it when we believe we are poverty-stricken, ugly, unlovable, and powerless. If we believe such lies, we allow ourselves to be disempowered to shift atmospheres. Instead we will be more self-centered and concerned about what people think or what we fear the enemy might be doing to us rather than tuning into what God would like us to do in the given situation.

When we believe the truth about who God says we are, nothing can stop us!

REFLECTION QUESTIONS

Look up some Scripture verses about who you are. Pick one to write out here and write on your bathroom mirror or other visible place to remind yourself of the truth.

Eph 2:6, 10 seated in heavenly places w/ Christ
I am His Workmanship, His poem, His work of ART
Luke 10:19
Behold I give you the authority to trample on serpents and scorpions and over all power of the enemy and nothing shall by no means hurt you!

Ask Father God for a few words that describe you. Write down what He says.

His Poem, His Work of Art

On the darkest days when I feel in Adequate,
unloved &
unworthy
I remember whose daughter I am
and I straighten My Crown!!

EMPOWERMENT PRAYER

Father God, thank You for adopting me as Your child! I know that who I am in You is amazing, but sometimes I don't feel that way. Would You remind me of who You say that I am? Thank You for Your supernatural encouragement that comes in so many different forms. Help me to recognize all the ways that You are telling me You love me today.

DAY EIGHT

BELIEVING THE TRUTH ABOUT OTHERS

Love bears all things [regardless of what comes], believes all things [looking for the best in each one], hopes all things [remaining steadfast during difficult times], endures all things [without weakening] (1 Corinthians 13:7 AMP).

WHEN YOU BELIEVE LIES ABOUT OTHERS, IT CAUSES YOU TO FIGHT THEM AND NOT THE SPIRIT REALM.

Another tactic of the enemy is to trick us into believing lies about other people. Mostly this will manifest in our belief system about their intentions toward us. For example, maybe someone didn't say "hi" and you felt hurt, causing you to get offended and think they intentionally snubbed you. Perhaps they didn't recognize you or they just had something else on their mind. The first step in being unoffendable is choosing to believe the best in other people instead of the worst (see 1 Cor. 13:7). A way to recognize the enemy's schemes is when you find yourself thinking negatively about someone, you can ask God if you believe a lie about them. If you do, you can take care of the issue with God.

There is the possibility that the person actually does have some issues and it isn't your perception that is skewed. But even if they do have problems and are partnering with sin and demonic broadcasts, you still have a choice to love the person and see through their behavior. Sometimes it can be hard to see past a person's faults, but with God's grace anything is possible. Even if the person is spewing lies and hateful words toward you, underneath all the mess is a wounded person who desperately needs God's love.

When we choose to believe the best about someone (regardless of their behavior), we partner with God's truth and deposit goodness into them. When we believe lies about another person, or focus all our attention on their negative behavior, we assign them the role as our enemy instead of waging spiritual warfare and going after the real threat.

Say you feel rejected by someone who doesn't seem to acknowledge you. There could be many reasons you're feeling this way, but ask God to show you the truth about you and the person. He may show you that they are afraid of you because you are a leader and they have been hurt by leaders in the past. Once you understand this, you can have empathy for the person and not take offense at their lack of interaction. You can also pray that God heals their place of hurt. No one else needs to know of this process (unless you feel the Lord directing you to discuss it with the person or your spiritual leader). Rather than to agree with the offense, pray for the individual—thereby helping them to tear down strongholds. When that person receives breakthrough, who knows what sort of effect it might have?

REFLECTION QUESTIONS

Is there a person who has been rubbing you the wrong way? Ask God if there is a lie you've been believing about them. Ask Him what the source of this negative feeling is. Now ask God to forgive you for believing the worst (if that is what He showed you) and ask God what the truth is about the person. Write down the good things He tells you.

Its just the enemy's arrows & my being negative
am praying for forgiveness of stinking thinking

Ask God to highlight someone He wants you to encourage this week. Ask Him what the truth is about that person. Write down what He shows/tells you. Say a prayer for them, too. Be sure to share with them what you feel would be appropriate in the next few days.

EMPOWERMENT PRAYER

Father God, in my journey toward shifting atmospheres, help me to always believe the best in people. I don't want to get caught up in pettiness or arguments. I want Your love to show through me and affect the atmosphere. Show me when I am believing lies about people and correct me by telling me the truth about who You say they are. I'm sorry for the times I've just looked at the surface level. I repent and I choose to believe the best in others!

DAY NINE

Believing the Truth About God

He who dwells in the shelter of the Most High will abide in the shadow of the Almighty. I will say to the Lord, "My refuge and my fortress, my God, in whom I trust" (Psalm 91:1-2).

Lies we believe about God cause us to go to the extreme of self-sufficiency or self-pity.

Another tactic of the enemy is getting us to believe lies about God. If we feel like God is not for us, it can cause us to embrace lies like self-sufficiency and self-pity. By partnering with these, we become more susceptible to the enemy's attacks.

There are many ways we can stay grounded in the truth of who God is. One is to remind ourselves of what the Word says. Psalm 91 is about God's protection and we can encourage ourselves in His protective nature when we read this psalm. Romans 8:31 says, *"If God is for us, who can be against us?"* Psalm 145:8-9 reminds us that, *"The Lord is gracious and merciful; slow to anger and great in lovingkindness. The Lord is good to all, and His mercies are over all His works"* (NASB).

The enemy wants us to doubt God's love and protection, so that we don't turn to Him in our time of need. God is the source of our power over the enemy. When our connection is weak so will be our resistance to the enemy. God's voice should always be guiding us, so we must maintain our connection with Him at any cost. The sooner we recognize the enemy's lies, the faster we can renounce them and declare God's truth!

REFLECTION QUESTIONS

What lies about God have you believed or been tempted to believe in the past? What lies about God do you feel are a current temptation for you to believe?

What are some truths from Scripture about God you want to meditate on today?

Psm 34:8
Psm 84:11

EMPOWERMENT PRAYER

Father God, thank You for being for me. You never leave me and never give up on me. Thank You for being an ever-present help in times of trouble. You are all-powerful and full of compassion. I don't want to believe any lies about You. Remind me of Your truth today. You are always good and I don't ever want to forget it!

DAY TEN

FORGIVENESS UNLOCKS THE PRISON DOOR

In anger his master handed him over to the jailers to be tortured, until he should pay back all he owed. "This is how my heavenly Father will treat each of you unless you forgive your brother or sister from your heart" (Matthew 18:34-35 NIV).

UNFORGIVENESS KEEPS US IN PRISON; FORGIVENESS SETS US FREE.

As we become aware of various lies we believe about ourselves, others, and God, we're going to see that in some cases we are holding on to unforgiveness. People aren't perfect and the fact that they sometimes partner with the enemy's broadcasts can cause us pain and disappointment. The enemy's ploy is to get us to start believing lies based on what we've experienced and to harbor unforgiveness toward others.

As we read in Matthew 18:21-35, when we don't forgive we are kept in bondage. Once we forgive, the prison door opens and the enemy no longer has the right to harass us. A lie we might believe is that our unforgiveness punishes the person we are angry with and brings justice to the wrong they did. In truth, unforgiveness does neither. It only harms us. Justice is not ours to bring; it is up to Jesus.

Once we surrender our ill feelings toward someone and choose to forgive them, a spiritual exchange happens. When we relinquish unforgiveness, the prison we were in becomes unlocked, the heavy yoke is lifted, and we can breathe the fresh air again. This is how we are meant to live, not under a yoke of bondage, but light and free.

We may experience times in our lives where we struggle with unforgiveness. Unfortunately, it isn't a once and done deal. As long as we interact with imperfect people, we are going to have to keep forgiving them in order to stay free. By God's grace, we can do it and receive freedom!

REFLECTION QUESTIONS

Ask God if you are in prison because of harboring unforgiveness. If you hear "yes" ask Him who you need to forgive. Take some time to work through this and ask God what He has for you in exchange. Write down what He tells you.

How does it feel to be free from unforgiveness? Have you ever felt relief when you have forgiven in the past or do you feel relief right now?

EMPOWERMENT PRAYER

Jesus, thank You for paying the price for my sins and forgiving me so I could be free. I don't want to be ungrateful and hold other people's sins against them. Help me to stay free from any lies and to stay out of the prison of unforgiveness. When I am tempted to hold unforgiveness toward someone, remind me of the price You paid for my redemption so that I can be quick to forgive.

Stop

SESSION THREE

WEAPONS OF OUR WARFARE

For the weapons of our warfare are not of the flesh but have divine power to destroy strongholds. We destroy arguments and every lofty opinion raised against the knowledge of God, and take every thought captive to obey Christ (2 Corinthians 10:4-5).

Although there is enemy fire and casualties happening all around us in the spirit, the way we protect ourselves and fight back isn't by using our own power or words or any physical weapons. The weapons that we use are unseen, just like the spiritual battles are unseen. In this session, we are going to find out what some of these powerful weapons are, and how we can use them to wage battle.

SUMMARY

In the last session, we learned about the tactics of the enemy. Recognizing the schemes of the devil is crucial to victorious spiritual warfare. In this session, we'll learn what it looks like to use *"divine power to destroy strongholds"* (2 Cor. 10:4). Dawna explains five weapons of spiritual warfare that we can use to thwart the attacks of the enemy: the Word of God, worship, prayer, the fruit of the Spirit, and obedience. There are many ways to use each one, so get ready to be even more equipped for battle!

WEEK 3

Video Listening Guide

Weapons of our warfare are not of the flesh.

They are:

- Word of God
- Worship
- Prayer keeps us seated
- Embracing the fruit of the Holy Spirit: love, Joy, peace, patience, Kindness, goodness, faithfulness, gentleness, and self-control.
- Obedience

The three seats of motivation in man's heart are: fear, love, and selfish ambition.

It is important that we pray from the right seat, the seat of love.

SESSION 3

Discussion Questions

1. This session was all about spiritual weapons of warfare. Why do you think we don't always view things from a spiritual perspective when we encounter resistance? What are some common responses you have that are not spiritual?

2. The first weapon of warfare is the Word of God, in other words, the Bible. What are some ways we can use the Word of God against the enemy?

3. The second weapon of warfare is worship. Dawna shared a story about her singing a worship song when a demon was harassing her friend and it left. What are some ideas on how you can use the weapon of worship to defeat the enemy or stories you have about worship shifting the atmosphere?

4. Dawna says, "Worship displaces the demonic, confuses them. Why? Because they are under a fallen worship leader. And when real worship happens they're confounded." Who can explain this reasoning?

5. The third weapon of warfare is prayer. Does anyone want to share a story about how a situation was changed due to divine intervention after someone prayed?

6. The fourth weapon of warfare is embracing the fruit of the Holy Spirit: love, joy, peace, patience, kindness, goodness, faithfulness, gentleness, and self-control (see Gal. 5:22-23). Dawna shared a story of her son Cory laughing in a Sozo session when a demon started to talk through a lady, and then the demon and the woman's headache left. Do you have any stories or examples of how we can use the fruit of the Spirit to defeat the enemy?

7. The fifth weapon of warfare is obedience. Obedience can be submitting to someone in authority over you and doing what they say, or it could be obeying what the Word of God says in the midst of temptation. Do you have a story of when you obeyed (either a person or God) or when someone under your authority obeyed and it turned out well?

GOAL

The goal of this activation is to uncover what is holding us back from wielding the weapon of obedience. After we forgive and repent, we can pick it back up again and use it in a healthy way with healthy people. We also want to start intentionally using weapons that God prompts us to use.

ACTIVATION

Freeing Ourselves to Use the Weapon of Obedience

We're going to work through the prayer Dawna led us through at the end of this session more slowly to identify if anything is preventing us from using the weapon of obedience.

Ask, *"Jesus, have I given up the weapon of obedience because of harm? If so, why?"*

If He shows you some people to forgive, pray this:

> *"Father God, I choose to forgive people in my life who have harmed me through control, manipulation, and fear. I have put down my weapon of obedience because I misunderstood its power and I didn't want to use it with unhealthy people. Holy Spirit, will You train me how to start practicing with this weapon with whom it is safe to obey so that I can take it back to powerfully tear down strongholds? In Jesus's name, amen."*

Ask, *"Holy Spirit, what other weapon of warfare do you want me to practice wielding this week? What will that look like?"*

Write down what He says to you.

Partner up with one other person and share what weapon God said He would like you to practice wielding this week. Be intentional to ask your partner the following week if he/she used this weapon and how well it worked.

DAY ELEVEN

THE WEAPON OF THE WORD OF GOD

For the word of God is alive and active. Sharper than any double-edged sword, it penetrates even to dividing soul and spirit, joints and marrow; it judges the thoughts and attitudes of the heart (Hebrews 4:12 NIV).

THE WORD OF GOD IS OUR SWORD OF THE SPIRIT.

Our first weapon of warfare is the Word of God, the Bible. As we know, the Word of God is not simply words on pages. It is living and active because it is God-breathed (see 2 Tim. 3:16-17). How many times have you read the Word and it speaks directly to what you've been pondering? Or have you ever been going along your merry way and suddenly you read a verse and feel convicted?

As Hebrews 4:12 says, the Word of God is *"sharper than any double-edged sword, it penetrates even to dividing soul and spirit, joints and marrow; it judges the thoughts and attitudes of the heart"* (NIV). The Bible isn't meant to just inspire and encourage us, it is also meant to keep us on track for who God wants us to be. This is why we can read the Word and feel the Holy Spirit pointing out issues in our life. As long as we submit to these convictions and repent, life will go well for us. If we feel convicted but decide we don't need to change, we become callous to the Word of God. As mentioned before, the more free we are from sin and lies, the more discerning we will be with the atmosphere around us.

In addition to the Word keeping us in line with God's standard, it also helps us refute lies and declare truth. In later sessions, we'll learn how to shift atmospheres over physical locations. Declaring Scripture is one of the best ways to bring about this positive change.

REFLECTION QUESTIONS

Ask God if there is any place in your life that isn't lining up with the Word of God. Take time to repent if needed. Write down what needs to change.

Think of a situation in your life that needs to be shifted. Search for a Scripture that speaks to it and declare it over that situation. Write down the verse and make it into a declaration here.

EMPOWERMENT PRAYER

God, thank You for giving us Your Word. It is amazing how alive and active it is. I give You permission to penetrate my thoughts and heart attitudes anytime with the sword of the Spirit. I want to be free from any entanglement from lies and sin. Teach me how to use this weapon effectively against the enemy and to bring positive change to the world around me. You're the best teacher and I want to learn from You!

DAY TWELVE

The Weapon of Worship

After consulting the people, Jehoshaphat appointed men to sing to the Lord and to praise him for the splendor of his holiness as they went out at the head of the army, saying: "Give thanks to the Lord, for his love endures forever." As they began to sing and praise, the Lord set ambushes against the men of Ammon and Moab and Mount Seir who were invading Judah, and they were defeated (2 Chronicles 20:21-22 NIV).

Worship confounds and confuses the enemy.

In Second Chronicles 20, the Ammonites and Moabites were defeated as the worshipers of Judah went out ahead of God's army! This tactic I am sure did not seem logical at the time, nor does it seem rational today, but we can still learn a big lesson from this. When we worship, it confounds and confuses the enemy.

This can look like playing recorded worship music, or singing acappella, or having a worship gathering with a group of people and live instruments. It doesn't have to be in a church setting. It can happen anywhere at any time. You could walk down the street with worship music in your headphones or take a praise break at your workplace. There is no formula for how it needs to be done.

You can even make up your own worship lyrics and songs! One way to do this is to take Scripture verses and make your own melodies to it. You may have witnessed this in liturgical church worship meetings. It doesn't have to be musically harmonious to the ear in order to send powerful vibrations through the spirit realm, as long as the adoration comes from the heart.

REFLECTION QUESTIONS

Have you ever made up a worship song? Take a minute and write down the lyrics of a song you'd like to sing to adore the Lord. Then sing it to Him!

Ask the Lord for a new way you can worship Him. Write down what you hear.

EMPOWERMENT PRAYER

Father God, Jesus, and Holy Spirit, I worship You. I lift You high! You are exalted above any other entity on the earth or in the spirit realm. You are magnificent, beautiful, and all-powerful! There is no one else worthy of my worship. I give You all the praise and all the glory, now and forever!

DAY THIRTEEN

THE WEAPON OF PRAYER

With all prayer and petition pray at all times in the Spirit, and with this in view, be on the alert with all perseverance and petition for all the saints (Ephesians 6:18 NASB).

PRAYER IS A WEAPON OF WARFARE BECAUSE IT FOCUSES ON GOD RATHER THAN OUR PROBLEMS.

The third weapon of spiritual warfare is prayer. Prayer moves the hand of God on our behalf and those that we pray for. How many times have you prayed and seen God answer? The truth is that whether or not we see the result of our prayers, *"the prayer of a righteous person is powerful and effective"* (James 5:16 NIV).

When we talk to God about our situations, we relinquish control and give Him the honor of breaking through on our behalf. As we focus on how big God is and how mighty He is to save us, our problems take a lesser place. The more we pray and relinquish control of situations, the easier it becomes.

When we hand God our heavy burdens, He promises to give us peace in return. First Peter 5:7 says, *"Give all your worries to Him because He cares for you"* (NIV). Jesus said, *"Come to me, all you who are weary and burdened, and I will give you rest. Take my yoke upon you and learn from me, for I am gentle and humble in heart, and you will find rest for your souls"* (Matt. 11:28-29 NIV).

We should never feel helpless in any situation because we have access to direct communication with the Lord who is on our side!

REFLECTION QUESTIONS

Is there something weighing on your heart that you should give to God? Write out a prayer here.

My not hearing H.S. promptly

Think of someone else you care about who may be struggling at this moment. Write out a prayer for them here.

EMPOWERMENT PRAYER

Jesus, thank You for caring about what concerns me. Thank You for not being distant and uninterested. I also thank You for giving me peace and joy in exchange for my heavy burdens. I hand You everything in my world that is concerning me now. I receive Your easy yoke in exchange. Thank You for going to work on my behalf in all of these situations.

DAY FOURTEEN

The Weapon of the Fruit of the Spirit

The acts of the flesh are obvious: sexual immorality, impurity and debauchery; idolatry and witchcraft; hatred, discord, jealousy, fits of rage, selfish ambition, dissensions, factions and envy; drunkenness, orgies, and the like. I warn you, as I did before, that those who live like this will not inherit the kingdom of God. But the fruit of the Spirit is love, joy, peace, forbearance, kindness, goodness, faithfulness, gentleness and self-control. Against such things there is no law. Those who belong to Christ Jesus have crucified the flesh with its passions and desires. Since we live by the Spirit, let us keep in step with the Spirit (Galatians 5:19-25).

The enemy has no legal right against us when we embrace the fruit of the Spirit.

The fourth weapon of our spiritual warfare is embracing the fruit of the Spirit. When we operate in the flesh instead of the Spirit, the enemy has a legal right to harass us. But when we live according to the Spirit and His fruit, the enemy cannot defeat us.

The Kingdom of God is a higher reality and is more powerful than the kingdom of darkness. Light dispels darkness, so whenever we act in accordance with the ways of God, it dispels the manifestations of evil. For example, *"if your enemy is hungry, give him food to eat; if he is thirsty, give him water to drink. In doing this, you will heap burning coals on his head, and the Lord will reward you"* (Prov. 25:21-22 NIV). Even if we don't see the kingdom of darkness flee immediately, we can be assured the spirit realm is being affected.

Every time we display love, joy, peace, patience, kindness, goodness, faithfulness, gentleness, and self-control we are showing the world who God is and what He is like. People will be drawn to us because of the manifesting fruit of the Spirit. As people draw near, we point to the One living inside of us who makes the fruit grow. Christians who display God's fruit not only make life easier for those around them but excel at using spiritual weapons to overcome evil.

REFLECTION QUESTIONS

Which fruit of the Spirit is your strongest weapon and why?

Joy, peace, Kindness, faithfulness, gentleness

Which one is the one you could grow the most in? Ask God for supernatural strength to increase that fruit.

love, self control

EMPOWERMENT PRAYER

Holy Spirit, thank You for making the fruit of the Spirit manifest in my life. I'd be cranky, selfish, and exhausted if it weren't for You! Please increase all of Your good qualities in my life, and help me to grow in the areas You know that I need. I'll be happy to submit to the process, knowing that in the end I am going to look more like Jesus!

DAY FIFTEEN

THE WEAPON OF OBEDIENCE

Submit to one another out of reverence for Christ (Ephesians 5:21 NIV).

OBEDIENCE IS SELDOM CONSIDERED A WEAPON, BUT IT IS POWERFUL.

What comes to mind when you think of obedience? Does it feel good or bad? Does it seem easy or hard? How we feel about obedience is a telltale sign of whether or not we have had good experiences with authority.

Obedience as a weapon is powerful when we obey leaders and submit to God. We don't need to submit to just anybody. If a person or entity wants us to do something contrary to God's law, we don't automatically need to obey them (unless we feel that God is giving us permission to do so). We do need to honor those in authority over us, as they are there for our benefit. Hebrews 13:17 says, *"Obey your leaders and submit to them, for they are keeping watch over your souls, as those who will have to give an account. Let them do this with joy and not with groaning, for that would be of no advantage to you."*

Because God is always good, He will not instruct us to cause harm to ourselves or others. If we feel like He is telling us to behave in a manner contrary to His Word, then it is possible we are not hearing His voice correctly. We are all in process of learning how to hear His voice, and our past experiences with authority can influence how well we hear. If we've had a controlling father, for instance, we might hear God's voice as controlling because that is our paradigm for male authority. As we break free from lies, we can better hear God's voice and obey His calling.

REFLECTION QUESTIONS

On a scale of 1 to 10, how controlling was your earthly father? Does the voice of Father God sound similar to your earthly father's?

5-6

Is there someone in authority over you that you're having a hard time submitting to? Talk to God about it and invite Him to share His perspective with you. Write down what He says here.

EMPOWERMENT PRAYER

Lord, thank You for being good. I can always trust You. You know every hang up I have with authority, and You have the power to right all wrongs. Bring safe leaders into my life who are for me. Teach me how to wield the weapon of obedience with skill and ease. Thank You for teaching me how to use it well.

SESSION FOUR

SPIRITUAL AUTHORITY

Jesus came to them and said, "All authority in heaven and on earth has been given to me" (Matthew 28:18 NIV).

I have given you authority to trample on snakes and scorpions and to overcome all the power of the enemy; nothing will harm you (Luke 10:19 NIV).

We have been entrusted with spiritual authority through Jesus's atoning sacrifice. Fear and prior harm done to us can prevent us from fully utilizing our authority. As long as we are cognizant of this, we can continue to grow as powerful warriors for God.

SUMMARY

Jesus has given us authority over the enemy through our relationship with Him. Yet sometimes it doesn't feel that way. When circumstances don't turn out the way we think they should, doubt can creep in about God's goodness and the truth of who we are in Him and what Jesus paid for on the cross. At the end of this session, we're going to allow God to uncover any places that we've unknowingly partnered with unbelief so that He can heal them.

As we learn about different weapons of spiritual warfare, it is vital we stay in constant communication with God to know which weapons and strategies to use in each situation we face. Just because we have a lot of weapons or tools in our tool belt, doesn't mean we should use them all at once. God knows which ones will be effective in specific situations. He loves to communicate with us and He wants us to be victorious in every battle

WEEK 4

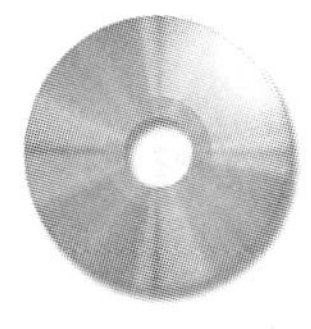

Video Listening Guide

If Jesus has been given all authority to overcome, He's given you also the authority.

Do you Know Him? Does He Know you?

Sometimes it's helpful to get support and get others to pray.

Unbelief can be blocking our authority.

Unforgiveness and bitterness hold people in their own prisons.

Who has the key to that jail cell? Two answers: you and God.

We need to move when God says move, and we need to stand and sit when God says stand and sit.

SESSION 4

Discussion Questions

1. Why do you think Jesus told His disciples, *"I have given you authority to tread on serpents and scorpions, and over all the power of the enemy, and nothing shall hurt you. Nevertheless, do not rejoice in this, that the spirits are subject to you, but rejoice that your names are written in heaven"* (Luke 10:19-20)?
2. Dawna says we should pay attention to the hierarchy of the demonic, not to be afraid of how big they are, but for what reason?
3. Mark 6:5-6 says Jesus *"could do no miracle there except that He laid His hands on a few sick people and healed them. And He wondered at their unbelief"* (NASB). Some people believe that faith has a tremendous part in miracles taking place and others say that neither our amount of faith nor the recipients' lack of faith should affect the miracle. What role do you believe faith has in miracles happening?
4. After lies are removed and demonic agreements are released, what are keys to the person staying free?
5. Why isn't it a good idea to automatically command spirits to bow or to leave places when you sense they are there?
6. When you recognize you are facing something larger than you have faith for, what do you do or what do you think you should do?

GOAL

To get rid of unbelief and increase our faith in God so the enemy has no place to hook us. To let God show us what attribute of Him in us is our strongest weapon.

ACTIVATION

Dislodge Unbelief and Identify Your Strongest Weapon

This activation is meant to help us identify and dislodge lies that are causing unbelief in our lives. We'll be going through a similar prayer to what Dawna led us through at the end of the video more slowly and let the Holy Spirit bring truth into places where we have unbelief.

Ask, *"Holy Spirit, is there unbelief in me?"*

Ask, *"Are there situations in my life that I have felt you won't come through?"*

Ask, *"What lie am I believing about these situations?"*

Ask, *"Jesus, what is the truth that you want me to know?"*

Write down what He says to you.

Pray this prayer:

> *"I hand to You, Jesus, any unbelief in this situation and I ask You to exchange it for the truth that You are all powerful, and that my weapons are divinely powerful for tearing down strongholds. Unbelief, go! Faith, come! Holy Spirit, take the place where unbelief resided so there is no waterless area inside of me for the enemy to attach. In Jesus's name, amen."*

For the next section of our activation, ask, *"Jesus, what attribute of you in me is my strongest weapon? Why is that?"*

Write down what He says to you.

DAY SIXTEEN

Do You Know Jesus?

Not everyone who says to me, "Lord, Lord," will enter the kingdom of heaven, but only the one who does the will of my Father who is in heaven. Many will say to me on that day, "Lord, Lord, did we not prophesy in your name and in your name drive out demons and in your name perform many miracles?" Then I will tell them plainly, "I never knew you. Away from me, you evildoers!" (Matthew 7:21-23 NIV)

Yes, you have spiritual authority, but do you know Jesus and does He know you?

As we discuss spiritual authority and strategies used to overcome the schemes of the enemy, there is something we must not forget—our relationship with Jesus. Although there is power in these principles of spiritual warfare, it is our connection to God that truly matters. As Matthew 7:21-23 says, it is possible to prophesy, drive out demons, and perform miracles without actually knowing Jesus. Kind of scary, isn't it?

God gives us authority, and the above scripture shows us that at times it is possible to have it apart from our connection with Him. Once we come to know Jesus and make Him the Lord of our life, the Bible describes our relationship with Him as like a husband and wife. Just like it is possible to be married and lose connection with our spouse, it is possible to be in a relationship with God and become disconnected. Of course, the lack of connection is never His fault; it is because of a lie we believe that is hindering our pursuit of Him.

People may not be able to recognize a person's connection with God, but the spirit realm can. When the sons of Sceva tried to cast demons out of a man, the demons said, *"Jesus I know, and Paul I recognize, but who are you?"* and they attacked and overpowered them (see Acts 19:13-16). Let's be people who are known by God and the spirit realm, as ones who are operating in power in direct connection with the Father.

REFLECTION QUESTIONS

When did you first come to know Jesus? How has your relationship with Him progressed since the time you made Him Lord of your life?

How is your connection with God now? Ask God how it could be better and write down what He says.

EMPOWERMENT PRAYER

Jesus, I don't ever want to operate in power apart from You. You are my source of power and it's only because of You that I have authority in the spirit realm. You are the vine and I am the branch. Let Your light flow through me today!

DAY SEVENTEEN

SOLICITING PRAYER SUPPORT

Again I say to you, that if two of you agree on earth about anything that they may ask, it shall be done for them by My Father who is in heaven. For where two or three have gathered together in My name, I am there in their midst (Matthew 18:19-20 NASB).

ISOLATION IS NOT YOUR FRIEND. DON'T HESITATE TO ASK PEOPLE TO PRAY FOR YOU!

As we learn to discern and shift spiritual atmospheres, we need to not navigate it on our own. Isolation and independence are not our friends. Community support is healthy and asking for prayer should be an automatic response to attacks against us.

We've talked about how powerful it is to pray both for ourselves and for other people, so asking people to pray for us is part of the same strategy to overcome the enemy. There is power when people pray for us. It releases reinforcements into the spirit realm. Jesus said, *"if two of you agree on earth about anything that they may ask, it shall be done for them by My Father who is in heaven. For where two or three have gathered together in My name, I am there in their midst"* (Matt. 18:19-20 NASB).

Some people have a special call to intercede and do this for others on a regular basis. It is good to have some intercessors in your life, so you can contact them to ask for prayer when needed. Others may not have a special call for intercession, but can still pray for you. Although it may seem weak and vulnerable to ask for prayer, it is of the utmost importance that we do!

REFLECTION QUESTIONS

How likely are you to ask people to pray for you when you need it? What do you think prevents you from reaching out and asking?

What do you need prayer for this week? Write down some names of people you can reach out to and ask for prayer support.

EMPOWERMENT PRAYER

Jesus, I don't want to be too proud to ask for help or prayer when I need it. If there is an unhealthy independent spirit attached to me, please remove it. You are humble in heart and I want to be humble also. Thank You for providing friends who care about me and won't hesitate to ask for prayer. Help me to reach out for support when needed.

DAY EIGHTEEN

FILLING UP THE VACANT SPACES

Now when the unclean spirit goes out of a man, it passes through waterless places seeking rest, and does not find it. Then it says, "I will return to my house from which I came"; and when it comes, it finds it unoccupied, swept, and put in order. Then it goes and takes along with it seven other spirits more wicked than itself, and they go in and live there; and the last state of that man becomes worse than the first. (Matthew 12:43-45 NASB)

VACANT SPACES DON'T STAY VACANT FOR LONG. THEY WILL BE FILLED!

As we learn about shifting atmospheres, breaking free from lies, and helping other people get free from demonic partnerships, there is a principle we must be aware of. Vacant spaces don't stay vacant for long. They will be filled. Matthew 12:43-45 tells us that when a demon leaves a person it comes back with other spirits more wicked than itself to see if there is space for them to return. If that space has not been filled with Jesus, there is a good chance the same demons who left will come back to torment the person. If that space has been filled, there will be no room for the demons to invade.

This is why we need to be steadfast with our freedom, otherwise we might be tempted to return to our old ways. If we expect to be tempted (at least once) after we gain our freedom, we will be prepared to say "no" and stand strong. When the demons see we are filled with the Holy Spirit, they will be forced to flee.

This is why we should always ask God for His truth and exchange it for whatever lies we have been believing. When we forgive a person for hurting us and renounce the lies we believe about them, we need to take a moment and ask God for the truth. This is why there is so much space throughout this study guide to write down what God tells you. Doing so allows truth to stick in your memory and fill up the vacant spaces with goodness.

REFLECTION QUESTIONS

Is there a lie or sinful behavior you sense the enemy has been presenting you with lately? What is the truth you can meditate on? Write down the truth here.

Ask God if there is anyone you know who could use some encouragement to stay strong against temptations from the enemy. What truth can you share with them this week?

EMPOWERMENT PRAYER

Holy Spirit, I don't want any vacant spaces in my life. I want to be filled to the brim with You! Fill me with your fullness and Your truth. Help me to stay focused on You so there is no place for the enemy to reside.

DAY NINETEEN

FOLLOWING OUR DADDY'S LEAD

Jesus commanded Peter, "Put your sword away! Shall I not drink the cup the Father has given me?" (John 18:11 NIV)

THOUGH WE HAVE BEEN GIVEN ALL AUTHORITY, WE STILL NEED TO FOLLOW OUR FATHER'S LEAD.

Even as we get more and more adept at using the weapons of spiritual warfare, we still need to follow our Father's lead. A good example was Peter's zealousness to cut off a guard's ear who was there to take Jesus away. It must of seemed a logical to Peter, but Jesus said, *"Put your sword away!"* (John 18:11 NIV). What seems logical to us isn't always the Lord's plan.

Just because certain strategies have worked in the past doesn't mean we should use them again. We need to stop and ask, "Father God, what are you up to? How can I partner to release what You want to be released?" Sometimes He might have us declare or shout or sing or do a prophetic act. Other times He might want us to be still, be silent, and worship Him or pray in tongues.

We need to move when He says move and stand when He says stand. We are not all knowing, but He is. We need to trust Him, obey His voice, and do what He says.

REFLECTION QUESTIONS

Have you noticed a difference when you follow God's lead versus when you initiate spiritual warfare without checking in with Him?

Ask God how you can partner with Him today to release what He wants you to release in your home, school, or place of work.

EMPOWERMENT PRAYER

Daddy God, I want to always follow Your lead. Help me not to be overzealous in using the authority and spiritual weapons You have given me. I want to be wise as a serpent and innocent as a dove. Help me to hear Your voice clearly and to trust what You're saying, regardless of how I feel. You're the best Dad and I want to stick close to You!

DAY TWENTY

BELIEVING GOD

And without faith it is impossible to please God, because anyone who comes to him must believe that he exists and that he rewards those who earnestly seek him **(Hebrews 11:6 NIV).**

BELIEVING GOD IS VITAL TO SHIFTING ATMOSPHERES.

In order to shift atmospheres, we must believe God is bigger than any demonic force we may encounter. We must put our faith in Him! In speaking about the spirit realm, faith is needed for us to operate effectively. If we don't have faith that God is working in our situations when we pray or that He can actually defeat the enemy, then we won't be very effective. Faith, although it is unseen, is vital to our spiritual authority. This is why the enemy strives to diminish our faith.

What happens when situations don't turn out the way we think they should? Do we let our disappointment diminish our belief in God's Word or character? Or do we let it go and stay strong in our belief that God can do what He says? The way we respond in times of disappointment determines our future victories.

The good news is that even when our faith is lacking, God can still perform a miracle. Jesus is *"the author and perfecter of faith"* (Heb. 12:2 NASB) and He is more than able to raise our level of faith.

REFLECTION QUESTIONS

Are there times when you prayed and felt your faith was lacking, but God came through anyway?

Is there a current situation in your life for which you need more faith? What can you do to remind yourself that God is more than able to accomplish what needs to happen in order for the breakthrough to come?

EMPOWERMENT PRAYER

Jesus, You are the author and perfecter of faith. Would You increase my faith so that I can shift atmospheres effectively? Bring supernatural encouragement to remind me of how big and strong You are. Help dispel my unbelief with Your faith so that I can be the warrior You say that I am.

SESSION FIVE

DISCERNING SPIRITUAL ATMOSPHERES

To each is given the manifestation of the Spirit for the common good. For to one is given through the Spirit the...ability to distinguish between spirits... (1 Corinthians 12:7-8,10).

Solid food is for the mature, who because of practice have their senses trained to discern good and evil (Hebrews 5:14 NASB).

Discerning spiritual atmospheres is a multi-step process. Having conversations with God and other discerning people about what kind of atmosphere we are sensing is a vital part of the process. While some people might excel at discerning quickly, it normally takes time to practice the steps before we are able to increase the speed in which we discern.

SUMMARY

An important part of shifting atmospheres is discerning the prevailing atmosphere. Similar to our physical senses (taste, touch, sight, hearing, and smell), our spiritual senses allow us to pick up information. Whether the topic of discerning spiritual atmospheres is brand-new information for you or not, we can all grow in the gift of discernment.

As you listen to Dawna share stories that illustrate ways we can discern, see if you can recall times that you have sensed the spirit realm in similar ways. Expect to receive an upgrade in your discernment by listening to this teaching and discussing it with your group. As you grow in this gifting, it will be helpful to pray with other like-minded believers. Pay attention to who God might be highlighting for you to connect with in this next season.

WEEK 5

Video Listening Guide

A negative spiritual atmosphere is a combination of the demonic realm releasing broadcasts____ and us partnering and creating a place for those broadcasts____ to land.

Negative atmospheres in our life come from the __lies____ we are believing and the hooks inside of us where __sin____ still has a place.

How do we discern spiritual atmospheres?

- _Smell____
- _Sense____ or feel____
- _See____
- _Hear____
- _Dreams____

You can have three voices in your head: enemy____, yourself____, and __God____.

Just because you pick up something going on around you that's being broadcast doesn't mean it's __yours____. That's why we have to know what we're free____ from.

When we sense the demonic around someone, it could be because they are partnering with it or it could be that they are being attacked____ by it.

SESSION 5

Discussion Questions

1. What is a spiritual atmosphere? What causes a negative spiritual atmosphere?
2. Although this session focuses on shifting negative atmospheres, what are some examples of positive heavenly atmospheres? Can you share a story?
3. Have you ever smelled the demonic or angelic? Can you share a story?
4. Have you ever sensed or felt the demonic or angelic? Can you share a story?
5. Have you ever seen (either with your physical eyes or in your mind's eye) the demonic or angelic? Can you share a story?
6. You can have three voices in your head: the enemy, yourself, and God. It can take time and practice to be able to recognize the source of what you are hearing. How can you tell which voice is talking?
7. Have you ever had a dream that gave you insight into the spiritual atmosphere? Can you share a story?
8. If we sense the demonic is attacking someone, what can we do?

GOAL

Practice discerning the prevailing atmosphere, getting feedback from other people, and asking the Holy Spirit what to do with what you sensed.

ACTIVATION

Discern the Atmosphere in the Room

In this activation, we want to practice the gift of discernment in this very room. Dawna says that one way we can become sharper in our discernment is to ask other people what they are sensing, and if it is the same as what you are sensing, that could be confirmation. This is not always the case. More than one person can be wrong but it is one way to grow.

What do you sense in the atmosphere in this room?

Ask the Holy Spirit where it came from. What did you hear?

If it wasn't a positive broadcast you sensed, ask the Holy Spirit what He wants you to do about it. As long as the group leader agrees, do what the Holy Spirit showed you to do (this could be for the group to do or just you).

DAY TWENTY-ONE

DISCERNING PART 1

Solid food is for the mature, who because of practice have their senses trained to discern good and evil (Hebrews 5:14 NASB).

AS SPIRITUAL BEINGS, WE PICK UP INFORMATION THROUGH OUR SPIRITUAL SENSES.

The first step in discerning spiritual atmospheres is to recognize that we are always sensing. If we aren't aware of what God's normal atmospheres should be, we won't see the need to shift the atmosphere or take further action. As spiritual beings, we pick up information through our spiritual senses. These senses are similar to our five physical senses. There are probably many more than just five, but for the sake of keeping it simple, we'll stick with that amount (plus one more). Today we will cover three. Because there are negative and positive broadcasts, there are examples for both types of information.

- **Sensing/Feeling/Touch**—This is one of the most common ways to discern an atmosphere. This could be a physical or more of an emotional feeling. On the negative emotional side, we could feel tired, angry, sad, lonely, or anxious. On the positive emotional side, we could feel energized, joyful, full of hope, thankful, and peaceful. On the negative physical side we could feel pain or heaviness. On the positive physical side, we could sense tingling, electricity, heat, or other types of sensations.

- **Sight**—This could be seeing something with our physical eyes that is actually spiritual (we call people with this gifting "seers") or it could be seeing something superimposed in our imagination. On the negative side, we could see a violent act or a sexual picture. On the positive, we could see an angel, a heart, or an image of Jesus.

- **Hearing**—This could be hearing something audibly, but more often it comes as a thought or voice in our minds. On the negative side, we could have a judgmental thought toward someone, an organization, or a condemning thought aimed at ourselves. On the positive side, we could hear a song with uplifting lyrics or experience loving thoughts about others and ourselves.

We will cover the three remaining senses tomorrow.

REFLECTION QUESTIONS

1. Is it a new idea for you to discern using your spiritual senses or is it something you do regularly?

2. Is there one sense out of these three you feel strongest in?

3. Which one out of these three would you like to grow in the most and why?

EMPOWERMENT PRAYER

Holy Spirit, thank You for helping me to spiritually discern atmospheres. Would you take me to the next level in my discernment so that I can take the appropriate next steps? Increase my spiritual senses to discern both good and evil so I can expand Your glory.

DAY TWENTY-TWO

DISCERNING PART 2

The natural person does not accept the things of the Spirit of God, for they are folly to him, and he is not able to understand them because they are spiritually discerned (1 Corinthians 2:14).

ONCE WE BECOME AWARE OF WAYS THAT WE ARE ALREADY DISCERNING, AND START PAYING ATTENTION TO WHAT WE ARE SENSING, WE ARE GOING TO BECOME MORE ATTUNED TO SPIRITUAL ATMOSPHERES.

To continue the topic of spiritually discerning, here are three more ways we can pick up information:

- **Smell**—On the negative side, we could smell sulfur, smoke, methane, or some other nasty scent. On the positive side, we could smell flowers or a nice perfume-like fragrance.

- **Taste**—On the negative side, we could taste metal or some other nasty taste. On the positive side, we could taste chocolate, honey, or anything else we enjoy.

- **Dreams in the night**—On the negative side, we could dream a natural disaster is happening or that someone we care about is being murdered or violated. On the positive side, we could dream that God's presence is strong or that something good is about to happen.

These are just a few examples of ways we can discern. Some people are more sensitive to spiritual broadcasts than others, but as Hebrews 5:14 says, by practicing we can train our senses. Don't discount your ability to discern because you don't sense atmospheres quickly. It can take time to recognize how you pick up information, especially if you have not been aware of this in the past. Chances are you have picked up information in these ways, but haven't thought about it this way. Once we become aware of how we discern and pay attention to our senses, we grow more attune to the presence of spiritual atmospheres.

REFLECTION QUESTIONS

1. Have you experienced all three of these ways of sensing? Write down some examples for each sense that you have had.

2. Which one out of these three would you like to grow in the most and why?

EMPOWERMENT PRAYER

Holy Spirit, thank You for the gift of discernment. Thank You for creating me with both spiritual and physical senses so that I can pick up information from the spiritual world. I want to grow in this gift, help me to become more aware of the invisible realm around me so I can successfully shift atmospheres.

DAY TWENTY-THREE

DISCERNING PART 3

It is the glory of God to conceal things, but the glory of kings is to search things out (Proverbs 25:2).

DISCERNING WHAT WE ARE SENSING TAKES PRACTICE, AND WE GET TO BE A DETECTIVE TO FIGURE OUT WHAT THE MESSAGE IS.

After we sense a broadcast, the next question is, what is the message we are picking up? Unless we hear an audible voice or see words flash in front of us, what we are sensing will require some interpretation. For example, if we feel nauseous or dizzy because of a spiritual atmosphere, we won't necessarily know why. It may be a mystery to us at first what we are sensing. In order to figure it out we may need to ask God questions. We can be sure that He will answer us. It may be the Holy Spirit whispering to us plainly, or He may just let a scene unfold before us in our mind, or He may have someone verbalize what they are thinking so we make a connection.

Sometimes it helps to ask other people what their telltale signs are for sensing certain atmospheres. Maybe a specific type of atmosphere manifests in their body a specific way. A couple of examples are sleepiness being a spirit of control, or sharp pain in the back signifying a spirit of rejection. We can also ask discerning people what they are sensing at any given moment so we can learn to decipher the messages hidden in the spiritual realm.

Discerning what we are sensing takes practice, and we get to be a sort of detective to figure out what the message is. Over time, we will notice patterns of certain sensations giving us specific clues to what is being broadcast. As we practice, it will become easier to quickly discern the atmospheres.

As we discussed already, there are sensations that are from God or His angels, not just the demonic. We need to find out whether what we are sensing is good or bad if we aren't sure. Tomorrow we will talk more about how to figure out the source of what we are sensing.

REFLECTION QUESTIONS

Are there certain sensations that you have had or are having on an ongoing basis that are still a mystery to you? Write them down and ask God to reveal what the messages are. Write down what He says to you.

What are some patterns of sensations that you have that you have found to have a specific meaning to you?

EMPOWERMENT PRAYER

Holy Spirit, thank You that You are the revealer of all mysteries. Thank You that I can always come to You and ask questions. I invite You to reveal the messages behind what I am sensing so that I can correctly discern and shift the atmosphere.

DAY TWENTY-FOUR

DISCERNING PART 4

To each is given the manifestation of the Spirit for the common good. For to one is given through the Spirit the...ability to distinguish between spirits... (1 Corinthians 12:7-8,10).

WE WANT TO KNOW WHAT WE ARE AIMING AT SO WE CAN TAKE AUTHORITY OVER IT.

Another part of discerning what we are sensing is finding out its source and the reason for its existence. In some cases, God might tell us right away. In other cases He might give us clues and allow us to find out the source. We can also ask other discerning people what they are picking up and God can use this to teach us. Finding out the source and reason for what we are sensing is important. Only after gaining this information can we can know what exactly needs to shift.

We want to know what we are aiming at so we can take authority over it. If we are hearing a controlling voice in our head, the source could be from several places. We could be thinking our own thoughts, picking up on someone else's, or hearing either God's voice or a demonically instigated broadcast.

Let's say we discern that we are hearing a demonic spirit of control. We should then find out why that spirit is there. Is it there because we have been partnering with a spirit of control? If so, we should repent and break any agreements with it. If it is there because another person is partnering with it, we can ask God what to do next. This will be tomorrow's topic.

REFLECTION QUESTIONS

Have you been sensing something lately and you're not sure where it is coming from? Take a minute and ask God what the source is and the reason why it is there and write down what He says.

Do you have examples of times when God has either told you the source outright or when He has given you clues and let you figure it out?

EMPOWERMENT PRAYER

Father God, thank You for knowledge, insight, and revelation. Thank You for giving me steps to discern atmospheres so that I don't have to be in the dark. Thank You for the times You have shown me plainly what it is I am discerning and where it is coming from. Thank You for the times You let me figure it out. You're such a good Dad!

DAY TWENTY-FIVE

DISCERNING PART 5

If any of you lacks wisdom, let him ask God, who gives generously to all without reproach, and it will be given him (James 1:5).

WE MUST ASK GOD TO SHOW US WHAT TO DO WITH WHAT WE HAVE DISCERNED.

Now that we have A) sensed something, B) figured out what the message is, and C) determined its source and reason for being there, it is time to decide what to do. As with the other steps, we must ask God for His strategy on how to reverse the negative broadcast.

If you feel like all these steps are overwhelming, here is a verse to encourage you. *"If any of you lacks wisdom, let him ask God, who gives generously to all without reproach, and it will be given him"* (James 1:5). It is God's pleasure to give us wisdom for every situation!

We'll talk about what to do when we discern regional spirits later. Here are two possible ways God might respond to our question of what to do with the information we have discerned:

- Intercession—God might want us to intercede privately for the person or situation.
- Confrontation—God might want us to confront the person about what it is we discern. This could be tricky, but if we go into it with a heart of love and humility instead of accusation, the person will be more willing to accept what we have to say.

It is also possible that God lets us know what people are dealing with so that we have compassion for them. In some cases, He might give us insight so that we don't succumb to the enemy's ploys through that person. But in our journey of discerning, we should not become suspicious or judgmental. Paul says it best, *"And this is my prayer: that your love may abound more and more in knowledge and depth of insight, so that you may be able to discern what is best and may be pure and blameless for the day of Christ"* (Phil. 1:9-10 NIV). Our highest call isn't to discern and overcome demons. Our highest call is to love God and care for others.

REFLECTION QUESTIONS

How do you feel about confronting someone if you know that God is telling you to do so? If you are scared, write down what scares you. Ask God for His perspective and write down what You hear.

In your journey of discerning, do you feel like you have a tendency to be suspicious or judgmental? If yes, ask God to shift this for you.

EMPOWERMENT PRAYER

Jesus, You are the source of all of wisdom. I call out to You and ask for more! I receive Your discernment, knowledge, and wisdom. Help me not to take action and do spiritual battles that I shouldn't be a part of. Give me Your heart of compassion for everyone, no matter what I discern on their lives. I want to stay in the place of love, and not judgment. Thank you, Lord, for teaching me to love.

SESSION SIX

SHIFTING OF ATMOSPHERES

For we are his workmanship, created in Christ Jesus for good works, which God prepared beforehand, that we should walk in them (Ephesians 2:10).

Do not participate in the unfruitful deeds of darkness, but instead even expose them; for it is disgraceful even to speak of the things which are done by them in secret. But all things become visible when they are exposed by the light, for everything that becomes visible is light (Ephesians 5:11-13 NASB).

We have been created in Christ Jesus for good works and it is our privilege to partner with heaven to bring God's Kingdom to earth by shifting atmospheres. Sometimes we get to do this by praying out loud, other times we pray silently. Sometimes, it will require confrontation and having brave conversations with people. As long as we communicate with God, He will guide us in what to do and when to do it. Any time we feel discouraged or afraid, we only need to call out to God and He will send angels to help us. Whatever demonic forces we are facing are no match for our heavenly Father and His angelic armies!

SUMMARY

Now that we have learned about recognizing prevailing spiritual atmospheres, it is time to learn the next steps in order to shift the atmospheres.. Of course these steps should be taken with the guidance of the Holy Spirit. Consciously deciding to not partner with whatever atmosphere you encounter and then sending it back to where it came from is the next step. After that, asking the Holy Spirit what to release in its place is the last step. Once you get a firm understanding of these steps, you can apply them to shift most atmosphere you encounter.

We will also be hearing stories of how Dawna approaches bringing up the topic of negative spiritual atmospheres with her family and friends to get their feedback and to help them get free from the demonic influences if need be. Let these stories be an encouragement for you to do the same!

WEEK 6

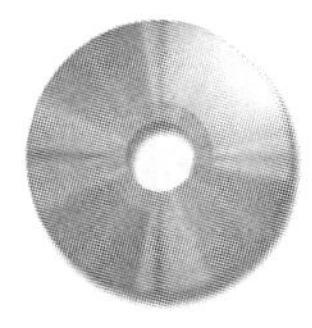

Video Listening Guide

The second step after discernment is renunciation.

The third step is displacement.

Most of the time shifting atmospheres looks like discerning it, renouncing it, and displacing it.

It is important that you learn what your normal state of being is so that you know that what moves you from your normal is not you.

Ask God to show you what is real.

Bringing things into the light helps people realize it is not a war they are fighting on their own.

(Love Gives
Lust Takes)
{Know my Normal}*

SESSION 6

Discussion Questions

1. The second step after we discern a negative atmosphere is renouncing it. What does that look like? Repent for partnering w/ it.

2. The third step after we renounce a negative atmosphere is asking God what to release in its place. What does that look like? Lord what do u want to replace it with?

3. When the enemy's broadcasts feel truer than the higher spiritual reality, what should we do? Seek the H.S.!

4. If you ask someone else if they are sensing what you are sensing and they say "no," what are the possibilities? What should we do then? Ask yourself some follow-up questions

5. Dawna shares about how she asked her boys if they were struggling with temptations when she had dreams or sensed an abnormal broadcast or atmosphere. Oftentimes they were struggling and then they were able to have a conversation about it. Can you see yourself doing this with your family, people you live with, or close community? With my girls

6. Why does it feel risky to bring things into the light by sharing what you are sensing and asking others to give you feedback? Because 2 are better than 1 - We lift up one another "Iron Sharpens Iron"

7. What are the benefits of bringing your discovery into the light? We learn from it to become better equipped to discern.

GOAL

To become more comfortable with the steps to shifting atmospheres.

ACTIVATION

Practicing the Steps to Shifting Atmospheres

Think of a negative atmosphere you encountered earlier today or are encountering right now. We are going to go through the steps to shift that atmosphere together out loud.

Say, *"I see you [insert negative spiritual atmosphere]. I am not partnering with you. I send you back."*

Ask, *"Holy Spirit, what do you want me to release in its place?"*

If you noticed an immediate shift and feel comfortable sharing, share what you sensed with the group.

DAY TWENTY-SIX

CHECK YOURSELF AT THE DOOR

Why, my soul, are you downcast? Why so disturbed within me? Put your hope in God, for I will yet praise him, my Savior and my God (Psalm 42:5 NIV).

IT IS IMPORTANT TO IDENTIFY OUR NORMAL STATES OF BEING. DOING SO ALLOWS US TO IDENTIFY WHEN WE ARE ACTING OUT OF OUR NATURE. THIS CAN SIGNIFY THE PRESENCE OF A NEARBY UNGODLY ATMOSPHERE AND AID US IN REJECTING ITS AUTHORITY.

Before we get into the next steps of shifting atmospheres, let's look again at how to discern what needs to be shifted. Being self-aware is key to discernment. If we don't know our normal state of being, we won't be able to identify those moments when we pick up ungodly atmospheres. If we know our normal state, then we should be able to discern what feels off or different from our character. Then we can ask ourselves and the Holy Spirit follow-up questions to discover the source of these signals.

It helps to be cognizant of how we feel throughout our day. If we wake up joyful, expecting breakthrough, but begin to feel depressed as our day continues, it might mean a change in atmospheres. If we don't "check ourselves at the door," we won't be as aware of the many atmospheric changes throughout our day.

When we aren't self-aware, we may be allowing the atmospheres around us to affect us instead of us powerfully shifting them. The Holy Spirit dwells in us and His presence will help us to influence any atmosphere we encounter.

REFLECTION QUESTIONS

How aware are you of how you should normally feel? Use some words to describe your normal state of being.

Joyful - Peace full, secure, calm

If you feel off from your normal state of being what do you do? After going through this study, what should you do?

Ask a family member & Check w/ H.S.

EMPOWERMENT PRAYER

Holy Spirit, thank You that because of You my normal gets to be peace, joy, hope, and love. Thank You for making me look like Jesus more and more. Even though it may not be always fun to encounter different atmospheres, thank You for allowing me to notice when my normal feels off. Help me to be more self-aware so that I can discern and therefore shift the atmospheres around me.

DAY TWENTY-SEVEN

RENUNCIATION

Sin is crouching at the door; and its desire is for you, but you must master it (Genesis 4:7 NASB).

THE SIMPLE TOOL OF RENUNCIATION CAN BE A LIFESAVER, SO DON'T BE AFRAID TO USE IT!

Renouncing ties with destructive atmospheres is the next step in shifting atmospheres. What this looks like is saying: "I see/hear/sense you [insert negative spiritual atmosphere] and I'm not partnering with you. I send you back." As long as we know the authority we have in Christ and we are not partnering with (agreeing with) the atmosphere, it will shift. This might not happen immediately but standing in the presence of God's truth always leads to breakthrough.

There can be real temptations for us to sin by agreeing with demonic spiritual atmospheres that we encounter. How many times have you been tempted to participate in gossip and complaining when a group of people are doing this? It is a real temptation, not only because you want to be liked by the people, but because there are demonic forces behind the words being said.

The key to mastering sin (see Gen. 4:7) is to recognize the temptation and to not partner with it. This can be challenging when we are feeling strongly pulled toward sinful behavior, but we always have a choice. The temptation itself is not sin, but willfully participating in it is. The simple tool of renunciation can be a lifesaver, so don't be afraid to use it!

REFLECTION QUESTIONS

Have you consciously renounced a negative spiritual atmosphere or temptation to sin lately? Does what you learned today help you understand steps you have taken in the past to not give in to temptation?

Is there an atmosphere you encounter on a semi-regular basis that can be a temptation for you? Write out a prayer that you can say out loud next time you face this temptation.

EMPOWERMENT PRAYER

Holy Spirit, thank You for enabling me to have self-control and to not give in to ungodly temptations. Help me to never let sin master me. I want to lead a sinless lifestyle that is pleasing to You. If there is any area in my life that I have been partnering with sin, please illuminate it so I can be set free. Teach me when to use the tool of renunciation so I can effectively shift atmospheres.

DAY TWENTY-EIGHT

DISPLACEMENT

This, then, is how you should pray: "Our Father in heaven, hallowed be your name, your kingdom come, your will be done, on earth as it is in heaven" (Matthew 6:9-10 NIV).

REPLACING THE VOID IN THE ATMOSPHERE WITH WHAT GOD WANTS INSTEAD IS KEY TO SHIFTING ATMOSPHERES.

After we have renounced negative spiritual atmospheres, we must fill this newly created void. This is called displacement. When we ask God what He wants us to release, many times it is simply the opposite of what the enemy was broadcasting. Other times it might surprise you what He is asking you to pray. Follow the leading of the Holy Spirit to discern what He wants you to release.

Some examples of atmospheres we might renounce and what we might release in their place are as follows:

- Sexual Sin | Purity and True Love
- Depression | Joy
- Greed and Selfishness | Generosity

- Violence | Safety and Genuine Care for People
- Fear of Failure | Unconditional Acceptance and Love
- Fear of Lack | Supernatural Provision and Trust in God
- Backbiting | Value and Honor for Others
- Comparison and Jealousy | Celebration

We release positive replacements by declaring them into the atmosphere. If we feel led to release a spirit of generosity, we could say, "I release the spirit of generosity over [a person or place], and pray that they would be inspired to give away their time, money, and possessions to people in need. Let them be so overjoyed when they do this that they will want to be generous again and again. Thank You, God that they are going to be a blessing to this city." We could also be led to do a prophetic act instead of specific prayers of declaration.

REFLECTION QUESTIONS

As you read over the list of examples of what could be renounced and what they could be displaced with, is there any situation that comes to mind that you are currently facing?

Ask God if He wants you to displace an atmosphere that you are discerning and how He wants you to do it. Write down what you hear and go ahead and pray or do what God leads you to say or do.

EMPOWERMENT PRAYER

Father God, I want Your Kngdom to come and Your will to be done on earth as it is in heaven! Jesus, thank You for wisdom on how to displace demonic atmospheres with heaven's goodness. I am open to creative ideas. I want to co-labor with You and see heaven's reality overshadow the earth's. May Your presence and goodness flow through me freely.

DAY TWENTY-NINE

The Reality of God

When the servant of the man of God rose early in the morning and went out, behold, an army with horses and chariots was all around the city. And the servant said, "Alas, my master! What shall we do?" He said, "Do not be afraid, for those who are with us are more than those who are with them." Then Elisha prayed and said, "O Lord, please open his eyes that he may see." So the Lord opened the eyes of the young man, and he saw, and behold, the mountain was full of horses and chariots of fire all around Elisha (2 Kings 6:15-17).

A key to shifting atmospheres is believing that the reality of God is more powerful than the seeming reality you are facing at the moment.

When we become more in tune with what is happening in the spirit realm, we must never let the reality of what the enemy is doing overshadow God's goodness. Like the servant of Elisha who was afraid when he saw the encroaching army, but then saw the Lord's angelic host, we must also be aware of the Lord's army that is for us so that we are not discouraged. The enemy would like nothing more than for us to be slaves of fear.

Although the enemy and his demons are real, God and His angels are more powerful. *"With God all things are possible"* (Matt. 19:26 NASB). At a moment's notice God can dispatch hundreds of angels to come to our aid. We only need to call upon the Lord and ask for help. Remember, the Lord is my refuge. Make the Most High your dwelling place so that no harm will overtake you. (see Ps. 91:9-12 NIV).

When you are facing difficult situations, it is important to remember God is on His throne. Your situation did not catch Him unaware. When we are able to keep His perspective, we find ourselves seated above fear with Christ in heavenly places (see Eph. 2:6). From this perspective, when it feels like the enemy is overpowering us, we can easily call to God to open our eyes so we can see His armies who are greater in number than those of the enemy's.

REFLECTION QUESTIONS

Have you ever had a keen sense that angels were helping you? Explain below.

Write down a couple of Scripture verses that remind you that God is greater than the enemy. You may wish to commit them to memory.

EMPOWERMENT PRAYER

Father God, thank Your for all the times You have dispatched angels on my behalf. Would You open my eyes to see the higher reality that those who are on my side are greater than those against me? I know that You are on the throne and are all-powerful. Remind me today that I am seated with You in heavenly places.

DAY THIRTY

BRINGING THINGS INTO THE LIGHT

But if we walk in the light, as he is in the light, we have fellowship with one another, and the blood of Jesus, his Son, purifies us from all sin (1 John 1:7 NIV).

CONFRONTING PEOPLE IN LOVE EXPOSES DEMONIC PARTNERSHIPS AND HELPS MAKE THE WORLD A BETTER PLACE.

One aspect of shifting atmospheres is bringing into the light partnerships people have made with the enemy so they can be broken. As we have discussed, the cause of negative atmospheres is often due to people partnering with demonic broadcasts. This "agreement" creates unhealthy spiritual cycles that most people aren't even aware of. As brothers and sisters in Christ, we need to be open to confronting others in love so we can expose any ungodly attachments. Doing so exposes the enemy's strategies and helps believers realize they are not fighting alone.

Most of the time we will have the opportunity to confront family members, housemates, or others we're in close community with because we have a relationship foundation. On rare occasions, God may urge us to talk with acquaintances or strangers, but never from a condemning place.

When we engage in brave communication, it is possible for people to deny what we are describing. If this is the case, we should honor their boundaries and not take the conversation any further. It is possible that our discernment is off and we are simply wrong. Or it could be that they don't want us to know about their struggles or are genuinely unaware that they have a problem. Protecting people's hearts is important when navigating this step. A good rule for knowing how to approach others is to think how you would like to be treated. Respecting people and their boundaries is key to advancing God's Kingdom.

REFLECTION QUESTIONS

Ask God if there is someone in your life you need to confront. Ask Him for a strategy on how you should approach the subject. Write down what you hear.

Ask God if there are people you should give permission to confront you if they see you partnering with or being attacked by the demonic. Write down their name(s) and make a plan of action to talk to them about this.

EMPOWERMENT PRAYER

Jesus, thank You for bringing the darkness into the Light so it can be dispelled. Thank You for Your blood that purifies us from all sin. Holy Spirit, You do such a fantastic job of convicting and comforting. Help me to follow Your lead and show me how to lovingly confront those You want me to approach. Feel free, Holy Spirit to lovingly confront me as well so that I can be spotless before You.

SESSION SEVEN

SHIFTING ATMOSPHERES OVER YOURSELF AND YOUR HOME

Now faith is confidence in what we hope for and assurance about what we do not see (Hebrews 11:1 NIV).

Finally, brethren, whatever is true, whatever is honorable, whatever is right, whatever is pure, whatever is lovely, whatever is of good repute, if there is any excellence and if anything worthy of praise, dwell on these things (Philippians 4:8 NASB).

Shifting atmospheres over ourselves and the places we live brings what we've been learning about to an even more practical level. As we apply our faith to shifting atmospheres, this will affect us and the people around us daily.

How many times have you wished the atmosphere in your home or neighborhood was different? How aware are you of what types of atmospheres you bring with you wherever you go? You have the power through Christ to bring change through your words, prayers, actions, and who you are. You could be one step away from seeing powerful transformation!

SUMMARY

In this session, Dawna addresses the need for us to become aware of the atmospheres we give off personally and the atmospheres we steward in our homes. As children of God, we should be promoting heavenly atmospheres. Dawna gives us simple tools to identify what is causing the negative atmospheres to develop so we can deal with them and invite God's presence to fill the void.

As we implement these tools, not only will we experience more joy and peace, but the world around us will be influenced by God's presence emanating out of us. Who knows what transformation will take place as a result?

WEEK 7

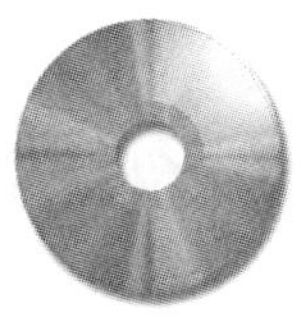

Video Listening Guide

It is important to know what atmosphere we are giving off.

Negative atmospheres we give off come from lies we believe and sins.

When you dwell on an atmosphere, it starts ~~broasting~~ broadcasting back out of you.

How do people respond to you? If it is negative, one of two things are happening: You're either giving off an atmosphere that they are responding to or they are listening to a Target against you. If it is the second one, ask God to dismantle their hearing ears to the voice of the enemy.

We should, as a family, be cheerleaders for each other.

SESSION 7

Discussion Questions

1. Why is it important to know what atmospheres we are giving off?
2. What should we do when we become aware that we are giving off a negative atmosphere?
3. Have you ever noticed that what you dwell on, you broadcast? Can you share a story?
4. Have you ever been inside of a house or building and noticed a positive atmosphere? Can you share a story?
5. What atmosphere do you want in your home?
6. What have you found to be effective to shift a negative atmosphere in your home? You don't have to disclose who or what was necessarily causing the negative atmosphere, but can just say what was an effective solution.
7. If you have already noticed your home giving off godly atmospheres and affecting people in positive ways, share why you think that is happening so that the group can get ideas for how they can do this in their home also.

GOAL

To identify what atmospheres we are giving off and to get rid of the root of any negative ones so we can start stewarding heavenly atmospheres.

ACTIVATION

Identifying and Shifting Atmospheres Over Ourselves and Our Homes

In this activation, we will be going through similar prayers to what Dawna led us through in the video and allowing God to speak to us about atmospheres we give off and give us keys to shifting those atmospheres if needed.

Ask, *"Holy Spirit, is there an ungodly atmosphere I give off?"*

Ask, *"Why do I give this off?"*

Ask, *"What do I need to do to make this right?"* You might need to forgive someone, renounce a lie, or repent for sin. Go ahead and do that now.

Ask, *"Father God, what atmosphere am I supposed to be giving off?"*

Ask, *"What do I need to know to partner with this atmosphere?"*

Write down what He says to you.

Ask, *"Holy Spirit, what atmosphere do you want in my home?"*

Ask, *"Holy Spirit, is there a lie I am believing about my household or someone living in my home?"*

Ask, *"What is the truth?"*

Write down what He says to you.

Ask, *"Holy Spirit, is there something ungodly that we have been doing in our home that I need to repent of?"* Go ahead and do that now.

Ask, *"Holy Spirit, is there someone in my house that I need to forgive? Do I need to forgive myself?"* Go ahead and do that now.

Ask, *"Holy Spirit, what atmosphere do you want in my home?"*

Ask, *"What do I need to know to partner with this atmosphere?"*

Write down what He says to you.

DAY THIRTY-ONE

SHIFTING ATMOSPHERES OVER OURSELVES PART 1

Finally, brethren, whatever is true, whatever is honorable, whatever is right, whatever is pure, whatever is lovely, whatever is of good repute, if there is any excellence and if anything worthy of praise, dwell on these things (Philippians 4:8 NASB).

IT'S WORTH TAKING A LOOK AT HOW WE SPEND OUR TIME AND ENERGY BECAUSE WE ARE MOST LIKELY BROADCASTING WHAT WE ARE FOCUSING ON.

As we continue on in our journey of shifting atmospheres, we must be aware of the broadcasts that are emanating from us. Everyone has a broadcast that is either good or bad. This largely depends on what we focus on. Someone who constantly dwells on hopelessness, for instance, will most likely spread that feeling throughout the day. This can then lead to people shying away from them in the public sphere, saying, "I just don't like being around that guy. He's always negative."

Here are a couple of ways we can partner with and broadcast negative messages. We could watch a certain TV show where the main characters make mean jokes about each other. If we aren't careful, we might agree with the mocking spirit behind the show and start saying mean things to our friends and family. Another example could be dissecting the latest fashion magazines and getting sucked into believing that beauty is equated with being promiscuous. The message behind many of these "sexy brands" is "wear me and you can be desirable too." It is hard to find a fashion line that promotes beauty without exploiting body parts.

How are we spending our time and what thoughts are we stewarding? Are we reading the Word of God and dwelling on the things of the Spirit? Are we daily worshiping the Lord or only on Sunday mornings? Are we growing in our relationship with God and partnering with Him to love and serve people? Who are we choosing to spend time with? It's worth taking a look at how we are spending our time because we are most likely broadcasting what we are focusing on.

REFLECTION QUESTIONS

Ask God what you should be focusing on that you haven't been focusing on lately. Write down the strategy for how to begin shifting your focus.

Ask God if you have been spending your time in unhealthy ways. Ask Him what other enjoyable, good activity you can replace it with. Write down both—what you're giving up and what you're replacing it with.

EMPOWERMENT PRAYER

Holy Spirit, You know everything about me. You know my weaknesses and You know my strengths. You know what I think about and what I am drawn to. I invite You to let me know if there is a negative atmosphere I am broadcasting because of what I am focusing on. Empower me to stop dwelling on what is ungodly and to replace it with heavenly ideas. Thank You!

DAY THIRTY-TWO

SHIFTING ATMOSPHERES OVER OURSELVES PART 2

Faithful are the wounds of a friend, but deceitful are the kisses of an enemy (Proverbs 27:6 NASB).

WE SHOULD INVITE PEOPLE TO SPEAK INTO OUR LIVES SO THEY CAN TELL US IF THERE IS ANYTHING NEGATIVE WE ARE BROADCASTING.

There is a place for others to share how they experience us. This might feel scary being that most people do not like to hear feedback about themselves. Change can be difficult; but if we understand the benefits, the cost of discerning friends who can give you insight into the atmospheres you are broadcasting. Part of being self-aware is knowing what broadcasts other people are picking up from us, both good and bad.

REFLECTION QUESTIONS

Ask a friend, leader, or discerning acquaintance whether they sense any negative broadcasts coming from you. (Feel free to say it differently if they have no idea what "broadcasts" means.) If they point out to you a negative atmosphere you have been giving off, talk through it with them and take time to reflect and ask God what He thinks is the remedy for you. Write down the action steps He gives you.

Ask a friend, leader, or discerning acquaintance whether they sense any positive broadcasts coming from you. Write down what they say.

Why do you think you project these positive broadcasts? Ask God also why. Write down what you think and what you believe God says to you.

EMPOWERMENT PRAYER

Father God, thank You for creating me. Thank You for friends and family that celebrate me well and who have my best interests at heart. Would You help my friends to be honest with me and vise versa so we can see healthy changes in each other? Teach me how to gently correct others, and bring friends in my life who are willing to do the same.

DAY THIRTY-THREE

SHIFTING ATMOSPHERES OVER OURSELVES PART 3

For you created my inmost being; you knit me together in my mother's womb. I praise you because I am fearfully and wonderfully made; your works are wonderful, I know that full well (Psalm 139:13-14 NIV).

AS CHRISTIANS, WE SHOULD BE THE MOST RADIANT PEOPLE ON THE PLANET BECAUSE WE SHOULD SHINE LIKE JESUS.

What we believe about ourselves, others, and God makes a big difference in what we broadcast. When we believe God is real and good, we are going to project a positive atmosphere of love and righteousness. However, if we have negative self-talk, we will project an atmosphere of insecurity and self-doubt. Overcoming some of these lies can be a process, especially if we have believed them for a long period of time.

The best way to find the root of bad beliefs is to ask God if there are any lies we are believing. Once we identify the lies, we can ask God where they came from. If we learned them from a person, we will need to forgive them for teaching us the value of the false beliefs. Then we must renounce partnership with these lies and break all ties from their influence. Next, we will ask God what the truth is and plant it into our heart. If His truth still doesn't feel authentic, we must go back a step and ask God if there are more lies we are believing.

Say we believed the lie that we are unattractive, and no matter how hard we tried to fix ourselves up we still felt ugly. We forgive everyone who criticized our appearance even our parents and others close to us who did not compliment how we looked. We renounce our partnership with self-hatred and receive the truth that we are fearfully and wonderfully made.

Now we get to start believing God's truth. We can write words of affirmation on our bathroom mirror like, "Hey good-looking!" We can ask God what He thinks of us when we look in the mirror. We can treat ourselves (ladies) by buying a new outfit or getting our hair or makeup done. God loves who He made us to be, and so should we! As Christians, we should be the most radiant people on the planet because we should shine like Jesus.

REFLECTION QUESTIONS

Are there certain parts of your face or body that you cover up because you feel insecure about them? (Obviously we want to cover our bodies in the appropriate way, but I mean parts of your body that are fine to show in public.) When you look in the mirror is there something you wish could look different?

Go through the steps above to uncover the source of your bad feelings. Forgive and renounce the lies. Take a moment to apologize to your body for not giving it the love that it deserves. Now ask God what the truth about your body is and write it down.

Ask God what some ways are for you to reinforce this truth and cement it in your soul. Write down ways that come to mind.

EMPOWERMENT PRAYER

Father God, thank You for the wonderful way You've made me, body, soul, and spirit. There's no one else quite like me on the planet! You are the Master Craftsman. I'm sorry for the ways I have not loved myself like You love me. Help me to celebrate the way You have made me and to love myself fully. I want to shine like Jesus and be a testimony for the world to see how good You are!

DAY THIRTY-FOUR

SHIFTING ATMOSPHERES OVER OUR HOMES

Greater is He who is in you than he who is in the world (1 John 4:4 NASB).

WE ONLY HAVE SO MUCH INFLUENCE OVER THE CHOICES PEOPLE MAKE WHO LIVE IN OUR HOMES. WE DO, HOWEVER, HAVE THE ABILITY TO FOSTER A GOOD ATMOSPHERE BY THE CHOICES WE MAKE.

Today and tomorrow we are going to take a look at shifting atmospheres over our homes. Unless we are single and live alone, we must learn how to interact with people in our personal environments so that our homes can carry an atmosphere of peace. Whether we live with roommates, family, or rent out rooms to strangers in our home, we have the ability to foster healthy atmospheres in our environments.

As you've probably figured out, not everyone you live with has the same standards as you do. Maybe you like to leave the kitchen spotless, but your kids leave dirty dishes in the sink. When we live with other people, we have the potential to be hurt and offended by them. When this happens, we have a choice of how we can respond. We can voice our frustration to their face or talk nasty about them to others behind their back. We can be inwardly angry and never say a word or communicate in a calm way from a place of peace and tell them how their behavior affects us and ask them nicely to change.

Our roommates, family, and guests bring spiritual atmospheres into our home. If they are partnering with a spirit of anger or offense, we could unknowingly partner with that spirit and be angry and offended while they stay in our home. If they are watching movies/shows that are sexual or lustful, we could be tempted with lustful thoughts. This is when it is appropriate to have brave conversations with them.

We only have so much influence over the choices people make who stay in our homes. However, we do have the ability to foster a good atmosphere by the choices we make. As we have discussed, the first step to taking authority over your homes is to recognize what atmospheres are being created. The next step, in case you discern anything ungodly, is to take authority over it. Shifting atmospheres in our homes is a great way to practice and will be beneficial to us and to everyone living in the environment.

REFLECTION QUESTIONS

Are the people in your home better off because you are living there? Is your presence influencing them to become better themselves?

Ask God if you are doing or saying things in your home that are not pleasing to Him. Repent if necessary and write out a prayer asking God to help you change.

Ask God if there is anything the other people living in your home are doing that is not pleasing to Him. Ask God for a strategy on how to approach the people you live with if they are bringing an ungodly atmosphere into your home. Write down what God says.

EMPOWERMENT PRAYER

Father God, thank You for the heavenly atmospheres filling my home. I ask that any realities disrupting Your will would be cast out and replaced with heaven's. I pray angels would stand guard over my house and alert me to any infringing spirits. Thank You, Lord, for blessing me and my family.

DAY THIRTY-FIVE

SHIFTING ATMOSPHERES OVER OUR NEIGHBORHOODS

How good and pleasant it is when God's people live together in unity! (Psalm 133:1 NIV)

IN ORDER TO SEE POSITIVE CHANGE HAPPEN IN OUR NEIGHBORHOODS, WE NEED TO BE AN AGENT OF CHANGE.

Now that we have done some internal work to shift our own atmospheres as well as the atmospheres in our homes, we can take it out a bit further to reach our neighborhoods. Have you ever found yourself thinking "there goes the neighborhood" or sa similar phrase? Or have you noticed certain positive or negative atmospheres in your area? Are your neighbors friendly or closed off? Do you know if they love God?

Unless you live in a perfect community, there will be atmospheres that need to be shifted. Remember, don't immediately confront the spirit realm without first asking the Holy Spirit what He would like you to do. As we notice changes that need to be made, we should dialogue with God about them and figure out how to best implement His presence.

Wouldn't it be amazing to be surrounded by people who love God, who are respectful, and who care for the community? Take some time to imagine what your neighborhood could look like. To see positive change, you may need to take action. If you want a family-like atmosphere in your neighborhood, you could host a party. Another idea could be to go on prayer walks and pray for your neighbors as God leads. As you dream with God, He will inspire you to take practical steps, whether they are outward acts or inward prayers, to shift atmospheres.

REFLECTION QUESTIONS

Ask God if there are some declarations He would like you to make over your neighborhood. Write those down.

Is there an atmosphere you feel needs to be shifted in your neighborhood? Ask God what you should do about it. Write down what He says.

EMPOWERMENT PRAYER

Holy Spirit, thank You for placing me in my neighborhood. I recognize that there is a purpose for me to be living where I am, and that no matter how long I live there I can be a positive agent for change. Give me wisdom in what to say and do so I can help shift atmospheres in my neighborhood. Point out people I can bless who need a touch from You. Use me to bring transformation to my neighborhood and my neighbors' lives.

SESSION EIGHT

Shifting Atmospheres Over Regions

To me, though I am the very least of all the saints, this grace was given, to preach to the Gentiles the unsearchable riches of Christ, and to bring to light for everyone what is the plan of the mystery hidden for ages in God, who created all things, so that through the church the manifold wisdom of God might now be made known to the rulers and authorities in the heavenly places (Ephesians 3:8-10).

If My people who are called by My name will humble themselves, and pray and seek My face, and turn from their wicked ways, then I will hear from heaven, and will forgive their sin and heal their land (2 Chronicles 7:14 NKJV).

You are powerful in Christ, so there is no need to be afraid of higher level demons. The strategies over regions, however, are slightly different than ones we employ over ourselves, others, and our homes. With regions, we place a greater emphasis on displacement. Just like we partnered with God to shift atmospheres in our homes, workplaces, and neighborhoods, we get to partner with Him to bring heaven's reality to earth in our cities, states, and nations.

SUMMARY

We've reached the final session of *Shifting Atmospheres*. In this session, we will learn how to recognize and displace regional spirits. There are hierarchies to the angelic and demonic realm and certain angels and demons can have authority over regions. When we pick up broadcasts from a regional spirit, there are certain steps we can take to release a heavenly broadcast. Dawna shares several examples of what this looks like. As always, we should stay connected to the Holy Spirit and ask Him for strategies in how He wants us to release the goodness of God.

Be encouraged, mighty warrior! You have been thoroughly equipped for the battle and are positioned to win!

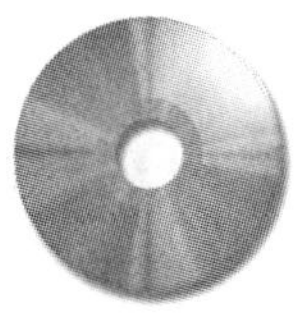

Video Listening Guide

There is an _______________ in the angelic and demonic realm.

One way to tell if you are dealing with a regional spirit is if you cannot change the _______________ easily.

The best way to stay under authority for regional issues: _______________ yourself, _______________, and _______________ anyone who partnered with the sin in that area.

One strategy to displace a regional spirit is by doing the _______________.

We shift the atmosphere by not _______________ with it and _______________ a military move of the _______________.

SESSION 8

Discussion Questions

1. Why do certain demonic forces have a right to be in certain places?
2. Dawna shares how she was led to call upon the name of Jehovah Sabaoth, the Lord of Hosts, when she needed heavenly reinforcements. Have you ever called upon one of God's names like this? If you do this on a regular basis, how have you become familiar with the different names of God?
3. Oftentimes we don't realize what regional spirits are over the place where we are from. Is there a spiritual atmosphere you've recognized in your home city? When and how did it become apparent to you?
4. Have you ever traveled somewhere and recognized a regional spirit? How did that come about?
5. What are the steps to displacing a regional spirit?
6. Have you ever done a prophetic act over a region or a piece of property? What did that look like? Did you notice a change in the atmosphere?
7. How do you feel about displacing regional spirits? Do you feel like it is doable?

GOAL

To recognize a regional spirit in your area and as a group get the strategy from God to release the opposite and do it.

ACTIVATION

Release the Opposite Spirit in Your Region

In this activation you will target a specific regional spirit in your area in the way God shows you.

Agree as a group which specific regional spirit you will target.

Keeping in mind the elements to displace a spirit (humble yourself, repent for ways you may have partnered with that spirit/sin, forgive anyone who partnered with the spirit/sin in that area, and release what God shows you in the way He shows you), pray out loud together as a group.

Ask God what strategy He wants you to take to release the opposite spirit into the region. Discuss this with the group and if possible, do it today. If it will require more time than you have, consider setting up a time to do it on a different day as a group.

DAY THIRTY-SIX

REGIONAL SPIRITS

Then he said to me, "Fear not, Daniel, for from the first day that you set your heart to understand and humbled yourself before your God, your words have been heard, and I have come because of your words. The prince of the kingdom of Persia withstood me twenty-one days, but Michael, one of the chief princes, came to help me, for I was left there with the kings of Persia, and came to make you understand what is to happen to your people in the latter days" (Daniel 10:12-14).

IT'S IMPORTANT TO KNOW WHEN WE ARE SENSING A REGIONAL SPIRIT BECAUSE THE STRATEGY TO SHIFT THE ATMOSPHERE IS A LITTLE BIT DIFFERENT.

When discussing how to shift atmospheres over regions, we should take a moment to discuss regional spirits. The same principles we've addressed throughout the study are still applicable, but the strategy is a little bit different. Regional spirits are demonic beings that are assigned to specific regions (like cities, states, and countries). An example of where we read this in Scripture is in Daniel 10. Regional spirits shouldn't scare us. Remember, God is still all-powerful and we're seated with Christ in heavenly places.

Recognizing a regional spirit (and not just an atmosphere) depends on how hard it is to "change the channel." By changing the channel, we mean the ability to reverse demonic messages and replace them with godly broadcasts. We might notice an entire region struggling with a specific issue. If this is the case, a regional spirit will most likely be the cause. Regional spirits are charged with seeding ungodly realities into the atmosphere. This is why entire communities, towns, and nations can struggle with epidemics like suicide, adultery, rape, or violence. The way we discern and sense the broadcasts from regional spirits works the same as with any other atmosphere.

We don't need to go searching for regional spirits, or any demonic beings for that matter. When they come across our path and we discern them, that is when we ask God what He wants us to do. The information we pick up is useful. Remember it is not sin to sense an evil spirit. We simply use our discernment to gain information to help us and others break free from its influence. When we recognize evil spirits that have been assigned to the region where we live, we can be extra vigilant to displace them under the guidance of the Holy Spirit. We'll talk more about how to do this in the following days.

REFLECTION QUESTIONS

Why shouldn't we go looking for regional spirits?

Why do you think it would be useful to know what demonic spirits have authority over the region you live in?

EMPOWERMENT PRAYER

Father God, thank You for teaching me about regional spirits. Even though there are most likely regional spirits over where I live, I acknowledge that I am not under them. I am under Your authority. Thank You for seating me with Christ in heavenly places, where I get to rule and reign with Him.

DAY THIRTY-SEVEN

PRAYERS OF REPENTANCE

If My people who are called by My name will humble themselves, and pray and seek My face, and turn from their wicked ways, then I will hear from heaven, and will forgive their sin and heal their land (2 Chronicles 7:14 NKJV).

PRAYERS OF REPENTANCE ARE POWERFUL FOR COVERING OURSELVES AND OTHERS.

In a previous session, we talked about renunciation as a step to do after we discern an atmosphere. When dealing with regional spirits, renunciation looks like repenting on behalf of ourselves or others who have partnered with its influence. It looks like humility, asking God to forgive us for any way we have come into agreement with its sin. What we are repenting for does not have to be the exact sins that people are partnering with, but it should be related in some way.

For instance, if there is a regional spirit that makes people feel insignificant, we could repent for any times we did not celebrate other peoples' successes. If there is a regional spirit of domestic violence, we could ask God to forgive us for any times we did not value the safety of our families.

People coming into agreement with a regional spirit's broadcasts gives the spirit legal right to be there and allows its influence to grow in strength. While we cannot make people stop sinning, we can do powerful intercession on their behalf and forgive them. This looks like praying, "God, I forgive anyone that has partnered with the regional spirit of [insert name of sin]." John 20:23 says, *"If you forgive anyone's sins, their sins are forgiven"* (NIV). This verse shows us how powerful our prayers of forgiveness are.

In addition to repenting, we should also make a statement that we will not fall into temptation and partner with the regional spirit. Not only are we repenting for what has happened in the past, we're making a declaration that we will not participate with that sin ever again.

REFLECTION QUESTIONS

Ask God if there is some sin you need to repent of that is related to a regional spirit. Write out your prayer of repentance.

Ask God if He wants you to stand in the gap and forgive others who have or are still currently agreeing with the regional spirit. Write out your prayer of repentance on their behalf.

EMPOWERMENT PRAYER

Father God, thank You for making a way so I can come to You through Christ's blood. I know Jesus's blood is greater than any sin. Thank You, Jesus for taking the punishment for my sin on the cross. Thank You for making me righteous, pure, and holy.

DAY THIRTY-EIGHT

DISPLACING REGIONAL SPIRITS

The people walking in darkness have seen a great light; on those living in the land of deep darkness a light has dawned (Isaiah 9:2 NIV).

AS WE MAKE DECLARATIONS AND FOLLOW THE LORD'S DIRECTION, HIS LIGHT AND TRUTH WILL EXPOSE AND DISPLACE ANY REGIONAL SPIRITS.

Displacing regional spirits is similar to how we have been shifting atmospheres. We get the strategy from heaven and execute it. This could look like making declarations or praying over the region what God directs you to say and do. It could also include us doing prophetic acts or good deeds so that positive broadcasts will be sent out.

As we make declarations and follow the Lord's direction, His light and truth will shine throughout the region. This will expose any evil regional spirits and displace their influence. We should be praying that as people encounter God's reality, they would lose their appetite for the enemy's schemes. For instance, we can pray that marital relationships and family units are unified so that husbands and wives won't be tempted to be unfaithful to their spouses.

We can take all of these steps and more to reduce the enemy's influence. Sometimes, however, it takes time for a community to transform. When evil spirits have been partnered with over a long period of time. If this is the case, it may take days, weeks, or even years before any major changes develop. No matter how much effort is required for an atmosphere to shift, we must persevere. Our prayers release prisoners and set captives free. *"Let us not become weary in doing good"* (Gal 6:9 NIV).

REFLECTION QUESTIONS

Ask God if there are any prayers or declarations He wants you to proclaim over your region. Write out these declarations or prayers.

What part can you play to displace a regional spirit in your area? Ask God and write down what He says.

EMPOWERMENT PRAYER

Father God, I want to join with what You're doing and declare what You're saying. Thank You for leading me in prayers and actions so I can bring Your Kingdom to earth in my region. Shine brightly through me so that the darkness will flee. Let people come to know You simply from experiencing Your presence flowing through me, whether I know it consciously or not.

DAY THIRTY-NINE

PROPHETIC ACTS

And Elisha said to him, "Take a bow and arrows." So he took a bow and arrows. Then he said to the king of Israel, "Draw the bow," and he drew it. And Elisha laid his hands on the king's hands. And [Elisha] *said, "Open the window eastward," and* [Jehoash] *opened it. Then Elisha said, "Shoot," and* [Jehoash] *shot. And* [Elisha] *said, "This is the Lord's arrow of victory, the arrow of victory over Syria! For you shall fight the Syrians in Aphek until you have made an end of them"* (2 Kings 13:15-17).

DOING PROPHETIC ACTS IS ONE WAY TO DISPLACE REGIONAL SPIRITS.

One way the Lord might lead us to displace regional spirits is through prophetic acts. A prophetic act is when we do in the physical realm an act that activates in the spiritual realm what God wants to release. An example of this is above where Elisha told Jehoash to shoot an arrow out the window as a prophetic declaration that the Lord was going to give Jehoash victory (see 2 Kings 13:15-17).

Sometimes God reveals the reason for why we are doing specific prophetic acts. Other times, He doesn't and we get to trust in Him and act in faith. Another example of a prophetic act is found in Joshua 6.

> *Then the Lord said to Joshua, "See, I have delivered Jericho into your hands, along with its king and its fighting men. March around the city once with all the armed men. Do this for six days. Have seven priests carry trumpets of rams' horns in front of the ark. On the seventh day, march around the city seven times, with the priests*

> *blowing the trumpets. When you hear them sound a long blast on the trumpets, have the whole army give a loud shout; then the wall of the city will collapse and the army will go up, everyone straight in'* (Joshua 6:2-5 NIV).

What God said to do may have seemed silly at the time, but it had amazing results. As we know, the walls of Jericho fell!

Prophetic acts can be fun or serious. Follow the Lord's leading and see where He takes you.. They can be lighthearted or they can seem intense. Following His guidance will shift the atmosphere and make good deposits into the region.

REFLECTION QUESTIONS

Have you ever done a prophetic act before? Did you notice a shift after you completed it? Write about your story.

Ask God if there is a prophetic act He wants you to carry through either by yourself or with other people. Write down what you hear.

EMPOWERMENT PRAYER

Holy Spirit, thank You for inspiring me to do prophetic acts to connect my faith to action. I trust that when I do what You say to do it will have an impact, whether or not I see it right away. I invite You to give me more ideas on prophetic acts so I can do them and shift the atmosphere over my region.

DAY FORTY

RELEASING THE OPPOSITE

Arise, shine, for your light has come, and the glory of the Lord rises upon you. See, darkness covers the earth and thick darkness is over the peoples, but the Lord rises upon you and his glory appears over you (Isaiah 60:1-2 NIV).

WE SHIFT ATMOSPHERES BY REJECTING THEIR MESSAGES AND BY RELEASING THE OPPOSITE.

Another strategy to displace regional spirits is to do the opposite of what the spirit is trying to convey. We talked about generous giving being a strategy to displace a regional spirit of poverty. If people are self-centered in a certain area, we could release the opposite by worshiping God wholeheartedly and by serving others selflessly. It doesn't matter if every person sees or hears about our righteous acts. We will be shifting the atmosphere and cleansing the spiritual realm regardless.

Here are some more example of how we can release the opposite in a region:

- Depression | Make people laugh.
- Hopelessness | Say what positive things are happening and make hope-filled statements.

- Sickness | Study biblical healing ministry and declare verses about healing.

- Gluttony | Exercise and eat well. Start a fun class to help others exercise and eat well.

- Isolation | Invite people to come over to your home for dinner.

We don't need to strain our brain to try to come up with what to do. God is all-knowing and can easily drop an idea into our hearts at just the right time. All we need to do is be available.

REFLECTION QUESTIONS

Ask God for something you can do to release the opposite in your region. Write down what He says and do it.

Now that we are at the end of the study, looking back, what has impacted you the most? Write that down.

EMPOWERMENT PRAYER

Father God, Jesus, and Holy Spirit, I love You. You are the giver of all good gifts, and I am eternally grateful. Thank You for all the revelations I have received throughout this study. Help me to apply it to situations that I face and to steward its information well. I am available anytime, so speak to me and I will listen. Amen.

Answer Key for Video Listening Guides

SESSION 1

Understanding the Spirit Realm

We need to shift what the enemy is saying.

A third of the angels fell.

When we forget there is an invisible realm, we start fighting against the visible realm.

Satan is not at war with God. He is at war with God's children.

In the Sozo world, the open doors are: fear, sexual sin, the occult, and hatred.

Unless a Christian believes a lie, he/she will not sin.

We need to stop pausing at the door of Jesus and boldly walk through both to Father God and to Holy Spirit.

Our normal should look like Jesus.

SESSION 2

Tactics of the Enemy

If the enemy can distract us, then we're fighting a battle that's not the right battle.

We must remember that we are seated with Christ and the very things that are attacking us are coming from an invisible realm that we have authority over.

Fear is one of the biggest tools that the enemy uses against us.

The enemy wants us to believe we are powerless against him.

The enemy wants us to believe lies about: ourselves, others, and God.

Self-sufficiency takes you out of the heavens with Christ and puts you down in the level of fighting man.

The enemy wants your worship rather than you worshiping God.

SESSION 3

Weapons of Our Warfare

Weapons of our warfare are not of the flesh.

They are:

- The Word of God
- Worship
- Prayer
- Embracing the fruit of the Holy Spirit: love, joy, peace, patience, kindness, goodness, faithfulness, gentleness, and self-control.
- Obedience

The three seats of motivation in man's heart are: fear, love, and selfish ambition.

It is important that we pray from the right seat, the seat of love.

SESSION 4

Spiritual Authority

If Jesus has been given all authority to overcome, He's given you also the authority.

Do you know Him? Does He know you?

Sometimes it's helpful to get support and get others to pray.

Unbelief can be blocking our authority.

Unforgiveness and bitterness hold people in their own prisons.

Who has the key to that jail cell? Two answers: you and God.

We need to move when God says move, and we need to stand and sit when God says stand and sit.

SESSION 5

Discerning Spiritual Atmospheres

A negative spiritual atmosphere is a combination of the demonic realm and God releasing broadcasts and us partnering and creating a place for those broadcasts to land.

Negative atmospheres in our life come from the lies we are believing and the hooks inside of us where sin still has a place.

How do we discern spiritual atmospheres?

- Smell
- Sense or feel
- See
- Hear
- Dreams

You can have three voices in your head: the enemy, yourself, and God.

Just because you pick up something going on around you that's being broadcast doesn't mean it's yours. That's why we have to know what we're free from.

When we sense the demonic around someone, it could be because they are partnering with it or it could be that they are being attacked by it.

SESSION 6

Shifting of Atmospheres

The second step after discernment is renunciation.

The third step is displacement.

Most of the time shifting atmospheres looks like discerning it, renouncing it, and displacing it.

It is important that you learn what your normal state of being is so that you know that what moves you from your normal is not you.

Ask God to show you what is real.

Bringing things into the light helps people realize it is not a war they are fighting on their own.

SESSION 7

Shifting Atmospheres Over Yourself and Your Home

It is important to know what atmosphere we are giving off.

Negative atmospheres we give off come from lies we believe and sin.

When you dwell on an atmosphere, it starts broadcasting back out of you.

How do people respond to you? If it is negative, one of two things are happening: You're either giving off an atmosphere that they are responding to or they are listening to a target against you. If it is the second one, ask God to dismantle their hearing ears to the voice of the enemy.

We should, as a family, be cheerleaders for each other.

SESSION 8

Shifting Atmospheres Over Regions

There is an order in the angelic and demonic realm.

One way to tell if you are dealing with a regional spirit is if you cannot change the channel easily.

The best way to stay under authority for regional issues: humble yourself, repent, and forgive anyone who partnered with the sin in that area.

One strategy to displace a regional spirit is by doing the opposite.

We shift the atmosphere by not partnering with it and releasing a military move of the opposite.

RESOURCES

Atmospheres 101 by Dawna De Silva

https://shop.bethel.com/products/atmospheres-101

Boundaries by Henry Cloud, John Townsend

http://www.boundariesbooks.com/boundaries-books/boundaries/

Brave Communication by Dann Farrelly

https://shop.bethel.com/products/brave-communication

Recipe for a Fear-Free Life by Dawna De Silva

https://shop.bethel.com/products/recipe-for-a-fear-free-life

Shirtless in My Offering by Stephen De Silva

https://shop.bethel.com/products/shirtless-in-my-offering

Someday When I'm Young by Cory De Silva

https://shop.bethel.com/products/someday-when-i-m-young

SOZO Saved Healed Delivered by Dawna De Silva and Teresa Liebscher

https://shop.bethel.com/products/sozo-saved-healed-delivered-a-journey-into-freedom-with-the-father-son-and-holy-spirit

Stepping Through the Door of Jesus by Dawna De Silva

https://shop.bethel.com/products/stepping-through-the-door-of-jesus

The Three Battlegrounds by Francis Frangipane

https://www.amazon.com/Three-Battlegrounds-Depth-Spiritual-Heavenly/dp/1886296383/ref=tmm_pap_swatch_0?_encoding=UTF8&qid=1497189728&sr=8-

Who do You Think You Are? by Ray Leight

https://shop.bethel.com/products/who-do-you-think-you-are-volume-1

Wielding the Weapon of Obedience by Dawna De Silva

https://shop.bethel.com/products/wielding-the-weapon-of-obedience